A FIRST ELECTRICAL BOOK FOR BOYS

Books by Alfred Morgan

THINGS A BOY CAN DO WITH ELECTRICITY

THE BOYS' BOOK OF ENGINES, MOTORS AND TURBINES

AQUARIUM BOOK FOR BOYS AND GIRLS

A PET BOOK FOR BOYS AND GIRLS

FIRST CHEMISTRY BOOK FOR BOYS AND GIRLS

THE BOYS' FIRST BOOK OF RADIO AND ELECTRONICS

THE BOYS' SECOND BOOK OF RADIO AND ELECTRONICS

THE BOYS' THIRD BOOK OF RADIO AND ELECTRONICS

ADVENTURES IN ELECTROCHEMISTRY

A FIRST
ELECTRICAL BOOK
FOR BOYS

by

ALFRED MORGAN

Illustrated by the author

CHARLES SCRIBNER'S SONS

NEW YORK

Many of the illustrations in this book were drawn from photographs and illustrations furnished by: The American Telephone and Telegraph Co., The Western Union Telegraph
Co., The Consolidated Gas Co., of New York, The General
Electric Co., The Warren Telechron Co., The Western Electric Co., The National Carbon Company, The Chicago, Burlington and Quincy Railroad Co., The Electric-Auto-lite Company, Motorola Semiconductor Products Division, Inc., and
Chrysler Corporation. The American Telephone and Telegraph Co. supplied modern telephone equipment to be taken
apart for information and sketching.

Much valuable information and many useful facts were
also furnished. The author is indebted for this assistance.

CONTENTS

v

vi

CONTENTS

A FIRST ELECTRICAL BOOK FOR BOYS

CHAPTER ONE

WHAT IS ELECTRICITY AND WHERE DOES IT COME FROM?

ONE of the first questions which any boy who is interested in electricity and the things which electricity does will want to have answered is:

WHAT IS ELECTRICITY?

Strange to say, you will not be able to find the answer here or in any other book. Neither will anyone, even a famous scientist or engineer, be able to give you a satisfactory answer to your question. They can only make a guess and tell you what electricity may be because no one knows what electricity really is.

Electricity is the name of something which no one has ever seen and whose nature is a mystery. You may ask, *but don't we feel electricity when we get a shock and don't we see it when it flashes sometimes?* And the answer is *no*. We never see or feel or hear electricity itself. We only see and feel and hear the things which electricity does. We can see the light from an incandescent lamp, hear the words spoken into a telephone many miles away, and feel the heat from an electric iron, but at no time has electricity shown itself to us. Even when an electric spark snaps with a flash before our eyes, we are not seeing or hearing electricity. We are only seeing a flash and hearing a sound which electricity produces.

In spite of the fact that so little is known about the real nature of electricity, this mysterious power is so useful that it is often called the servant of mankind. But this was not always so. Although you and I are accustomed to incandescent electric lamps, electric elevators, radios, telephones, and many other electrical marvels which help to make us more comfortable and which it would seem hard to get along without, there are people alive today who are old enough to remember the time when, with the exception of the electric telegraph, these other wonderful electrical things did not exist.

For a long time in the world's history electricity was only a plaything—just something to do scientific tricks with. That was because men had not yet found out enough about it to use it properly. It is hardly one hundred years ago that electricity was first put to work—when something useful was found for it to do and it ceased being entirely a plaything. No one knew much about the rules or laws which electricity always obeys before that time and so they did not know how to build machines for using electricity. All of the really accurate electrical knowledge of those old days could easily have been put into a book smaller than this one. Now it requires hundreds of volumes, enough to fill a very large room. The things which have been found out about electricity have become a beautiful science and the many different uses which have been developed for its powers are so widespread that every man, woman, and child has their way of living affected by it and has been made more comfortable in some way or other.

WHERE DOES ELECTRICITY COME FROM?

No one knows where electricity comes from any more than they know what it is. We only know that it hides almost everywhere and that there are several ways of bringing it forth from its hiding places. Scientists speak of producing and generating electricity but these words are a little misleading if they give you the idea that electricity can actually be created or manufactured. For that is not so. The whole world seems to be a great reservoir of electricity and by "producing" or "generating" we only mean a method of *gathering* some of this great inexhaustible supply together so it can be used.

Electricity can be brought forth from its hiding places in strange and unsuspected ways. Chemicals and magnets may be used and so can friction. The first electricity which anyone knew anything about was gathered together by means of friction. Whenever most substances are rubbed together, the friction between them brings forth electricity. Some materials reveal electricity when they are torn or broken apart. The actual amount of electricity which appears in this manner may be very small and difficult for anyone not equipped with the right sort of scientific instruments

BENJAMIN FRANKLIN
Proved that lightning is electricity.

to perceive but it is nevertheless there. Even doing such a simple thing as sharpening a pencil with a knife produces electricity. There are instruments which are so delicate and sensitive that they will measure the electricity generated on the wooden shavings as they are torn off the pencil by the knife blade.

WHO WOULD THINK OF LOOKING FOR ELECTRICITY IN A LUMP OF SUGAR?

But it can be found there if you know how. If you take a dry lump of sugar into a pitch-dark room and after waiting a few mo-

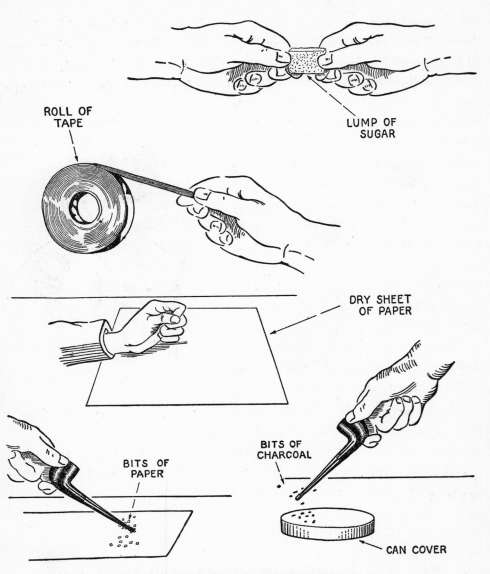

ROLL OF
TAPE

LUMP OF
SUGAR

DRY SHEET
OF PAPER

BITS OF
PAPER

BITS OF
CHARCOAL

CAN COVER

EXPERIMENTS WITH STATIC ELECTRICITY

If you break a dry lump of sugar in the dark, there will be a faint flash of light in the sugar. When a strip of tire tape is suddenly pulled off its roll, there is a faint violet-colored light where the tape is torn away. Rubbing a sheet of dry paper will generate static electricity. A fountain pen or pipe stem which has been rubbed will attract small bits of paper or charcoal.

ments until your eyes are accustomed to the darkness, break the lump in half between your fingers, there will be a quick flash of faint light in the sugar. Here is the explanation. When the little crystals of sugar are torn apart, electricity comes forth and it is this electricity which creates the faint light which is seen.

When a strip of tire tape—or electrician's tape—is suddenly pulled off its roll, there is a faint violet-colored light at the place where the tape is torn away. You can easily see it in a dark room. This light is also created by electricity. The electricity is produced when the sticky substance on the tape is torn apart.

ELECTRICITY IN STRANGE PLACES
Even a cat will generate electricity when you rub its fur with your hands.

Who would have thought that a lump of sugar or a roll of tire tape could be used to produce electricity? There are a great many other things besides sugar and tire tape which will do it. You may include a pair of slippers, a cat and a sheet of writing paper in the strange list if you care to. Have you ever slid your feet along over a thick carpet on a cold winter's night, when it was dry and clear outdoors, and then quickly touched your finger to the radiator or to the knuckles of an unsuspecting friend? [1] Were you surprised when the snapping little spark jumped from your finger tips. The flash of that little spark released the electricity with which your body had become charged by your slippers rubbing on the carpet. Leather belts rubbing against their pulleys often produce

[1] Rubber soles will not work for this experiment. Thin-soled leather slippers on your feet give the best results.

so much electricity that precautions are taken to prevent it in factories where an electric spark might cause an explosion.

In winter, when you are combing your hair with a hard rubber comb, sometimes your hair will stand up all over your head instead of lying down flat and if you listen carefully, a faint crackling noise will be heard. Electricity is showing itself again in an unsuspected way. It has been brought forth by the friction between your hair and the comb.

Even a cat will generate electricity when you rub its fur with your hands. When the weather is cold and dry if you are in a dark room, you will be able to see, in fact hear and feel, the sparks made by the electricity generated when you rub a cat. If you touch the cat's nose with one hand while you are stroking his fur with the other, a tiny spark will jump from your finger. It won't hurt the cat—it will only ruffle his dignity. After you have tried the experiment once, don't tease him any longer.

A sheet of paper which has been warmed before the fire and then laid on a bare wooden table and briskly rubbed with your hand will cling to the table when you try to lift it up by one corner. It is electricity, generated on the paper by rubbing with your hand, which causes the paper to cling to the table.

ELECTRICITY MAY BE A NUISANCE AT TIMES

In paper manufacturing and printing, a great deal of trouble is often caused by the electricity generated on the paper by friction as it passes through the machines. The sheets of paper cling and drag. Keeping the air damp in the pressroom is one of the means used in overcoming this.

When gasoline is poured from one tank into another, electricity is sometimes produced and explosions and fires have occurred which were due to this cause. The next time that you see a gasoline truck, notice the chain which hangs down and drags along the ground. The chain connects the tank with the earth and prevents electricity from being generated in sufficient quantity, when the gasoline is drawn off, to cause an explosion.

THERE IS MORE THAN ONE KIND OF ELECTRICITY

Electricity which is generated when two substances are rubbed together is called *frictional* electricity. It is also called *static* electricity from a Greek word meaning "standing," because it is generally at rest and stands still on the surface of things. Static electricity is not of much use. The electricity used for lighting our homes, for operating motors, telephones, etc., is not produced by friction and is not static electricity. It is not like static electricity because it does not stand still. It is produced by magnetism and moves in a current like a stream of water running through a pipe. This useful sort of electricity is called *dynamic* and *current electricity*. It is more important than static electricity because it is more useful. So is the electricity which is generated by batteries and called *galvanic* and sometimes *voltaic* electricity after Galvani and Volta, the two famous men who discovered how to produce it. Much more will be told about these other forms of electricity later in this book when we are through talking about static electricity.

WHAT IS STATIC ELECTRICITY GOOD FOR?

There is almost no practical use for static electricity except to teach young scientists and future engineers many facts which are useful to know. Thirty-five years ago, however, when doctors first commenced to use the newly discovered X-ray for examining broken bones or searching for bullets and pieces of metal which had become lodged in the human body, machines which generated static electricity were often used to operate the X-ray tubes. There is a much more satisfactory way of producing current for X-ray tubes in use today. Instruments called transformers are used. There will be more said about them later.

WHAT ARE THUNDER AND LIGHTNING?

For a long time the whole world wanted to know the answer to that question. We know now. It is static electricity which jumps between the clouds and the earth or between the clouds themselves and produces the flashes and crashing thunder. The snap and flash of an electric spark are miniature thunder and lightning. The terrifying flash and crash in the heavens were once thought to be such silly things as warfare among the gods and all sorts of other strange imaginary happenings until Benjamin Franklin proved that lightning is really a gigantic spark produced by electricity leaping through the atmosphere and that thunder is the noise which the huge spark causes.

The question that is now running through your mind is no doubt:

WHERE DOES THE ELECTRICITY WHICH CAUSES LIGHTNING COME FROM?

But unfortunately just like the answers to many other questions in the realm of science, the explanation is not wholly satisfactory because no one knows the whole answer. Scientists have satisfied themselves as to this fact however. The air is usually electrified, even in clear weather. The cause of this is not thoroughly understood. The sun's rays may be responsible. In fact all electricity may come from the sun. Electricity in the atmosphere collects on water vapor in the air. Little particles of water vapor, joining together to form larger-sized drops, help the electricity to accumulate and form charges powerful enough to crash across the heavens in a great bolt of lightning.

Scientists have tried to keep accurate records of electrical storms over large areas of the world's surface and estimate from the facts gathered in this manner that there are approximately 44,000 thunder-and-lightning storms every year and about 6,000 lightning flashes taking place in the earth's atmosphere every minute. So you

ELECTRICITY FROM THE CLOUDS STRIKING A POWER LINE

The unseen electric current in the power line goes about its work silently and invisibly because men have learned how to control it. There is much less energy in the crashing and flashing lightning but it is uncontrolled and so often makes havoc.

see there is a lot of thunder and lightning in the world all the time even though there may not be a storm going on where you are.

IS LIGHTNING USEFUL?

There is probably nothing in this world of ours which does not have its purpose—even lightning. Those alarming bolts of electricity which dart from the sky and often shatter trees and buildings and sometimes kill men and animals, have been found to have a useful result. They release chemicals called nitrogen compounds in the air. These nitrogen compounds are a very fine fertilizer. It is estimated that nearly 100,000,000 tons find their way into the soil every year and help make the plants grow. But lightning is not the only way Nature has of displaying electricity's strange behavior to us. We sometimes see what is known as the

AURORA BOREALIS

The Aurora Borealis, also called Northern Lights, which hangs out its beautiful drapery in the skies of northern latitudes, is some sort of an atmospheric electrical effect whose real cause is not known. Those who live in the southern part of the United States have probably never seen it. The weird spectacle sometimes appears in the skies in the latitude of New York. It occurs more often and is more brilliant farther north. It often happens at a time when the mariner's compass and long-distance telegraph lines are distributed by what is known as a magnetic storm. There is a coincidence between these mysterious events with changes which take place in the spots on the sun. We know a lot about this old world upon which we live but we don't know everything, and sun spots, aurora, and magnetic storms are some of the things which are not understood.

SAINT ELMO'S FIRE

It is really static electricity escaping from the ends of a
ship's masts and spars which produces this weird light.

As if these strange happenings were not enough, atmospheric electricity has still another little trick called

SAINT ELMO'S FIRE

Sailors are often very much startled to see a flickering luminous light at the tips of a ship's masts and spars at night. It was noticed for thousands of years without anyone knowing what it was until about one hundred and fifty years ago. It is called Saint Elmo's Fire but is really static electricity passing from the earth and through the ship into the atmosphere. As it escapes from the ends of the masts and spars a flickering light is produced. Saint Elmo's Fire differs from lightning because the electricity leaks away gradually instead of disappearing in a fraction of a second in one crash.

THE FIRST ELECTRICAL EXPERIMENTER

Our knowledge of the beginnings of certain sciences is very limited and meager. This is especially true in the case of the science called electricity. No one knows how long ago static electricity was first noticed or who the first person to experiment with it was. Of course there has always been lightning flashing around overhead but no one knew that it was electricity until about the year 1745. Although he might not have been actually the first experimenter, the first man to write about electricity, as far as we know, was Thales. This ancient scientist was born about the middle of the seventh century B.C. and might have been either a Greek or a Phœnician. No one knows which—neither do we know what he looked like. He lived in Greece and spent a great deal of time in Egypt. Judging from the things which the famous Greek philosopher Aristotle claims that Thales did twenty-five hundred years ago, he was one of the few men in those days who could reason for more than a few minutes without becoming very much muddled. Thales was a careful observer and an exact thinker—a real scientist at a time when scientists were few and far between. He did many brilliant things which make people still read and write about him almost three thousand years later, but in an electrical book for boys we are only interested in one of them. He drew attention to the curious power of a resin, called amber, to attract and pick up light bodies after it had been rubbed and *he gave the reason* for its strange behavior. Amber is the gum from an extinct species of trees which once grew along the shores of the Baltic Sea and which after lying in the ground for thousands of years, became hard and petrified. A great many museums have pieces of amber on exhibition which contain the bodies of insects imprisoned in the resin when it was soft thousands of years ago. The Greeks called amber *elektron* and used it for making pretty yellow beads for necklaces. It is from this Greek word for amber that electricity gained its name. We still make necklaces of amber—also pipe stems and cigarette holders.

Although a great many other substances will also generate static electricity and attract light objects when rubbed, it is a curious fact that amber and jet were the only two which it was known would act in this strange manner until the time of the famous Queen Elizabeth whom you read about in English history. Men had been playing with amber and jet for hundreds of years but none of them had ever thought to rub anything else and see what it would do until a Doctor Gilbert, who lived in Colchester, England, in the sixteenth century, discovered that a long list of other substances, such as glass, diamond, sulfur, sapphire, sealing wax, rock crystals, and resin, which he called *electrics*, would also behave like amber and jet when rubbed.

In these days of radios and X-rays when so much is known about electricity, Doctor Gilbert's discovery that there were other substances besides amber which would produce electricity, may appear to you to have been unimportant. But three hundred years ago it startled the whole scientific world and the consequence was that electricity drew more attention than it ever had before. Men started to rub all sorts of things with silk and wool to see what would happen. When enough different people start to think about the same thing it is bound to bring results.

Experiments which only a learned scientist could perform in the seventeenth century can be tried in the twentieth century by any boy who is interested in electricity. Things which were mysterious yesterday are often simple today because they are better understood. A great deal of fun can be had experimenting with static electricity without the necessity of spending a penny for apparatus.

This you should know. It will help to make your experiments more successful. Static electricity is a nervous, flighty thing. It is here for a moment and then gone in a jiffy. It is easy to produce but hard to keep. Much of this difficulty is due to moisture in the air. There is more moisture in the air during the summer time than during the winter. For that reason experiments with static electricity are difficult to perform in the summer. They work best in the winter.

AN EXPERIMENT MORE THAN TWENTY-FIVE HUNDRED YEARS OLD

You will not need a piece of amber to try the same sort of an experiment which Thales did more than twenty-five hundred years ago. There are a number of common things right at hand which will produce static electricity when rubbed. Instead of amber, you can use a glass rod, a stick of sealing wax, a hard rubber pipe stem or comb, or some article made of a plastic such as Lucite.

Any of these things will become charged with electricity or electrified if you rub them briskly with a piece of warm dry flannel or woolen cloth. A piece of rabbit's fur will work even better than flannel. You will not have to shoot a rabbit to get a piece of rabbit's fur. It is used a great deal for lining coats and you can get a piece at a furrier's.

Snip some tissue paper into very small bits, about as large as the head of a dressmaker's pin. Then hold a hard rubber pipe stem or a glass rod which has just been rubbed briskly with a piece of flannel or fur over the bits of paper. Bring it down slowly and just before it quite touches them, some of the pieces of paper will jump up to meet the rod. If you watch very closely you may see some of the little pieces of paper fly quickly away from the rod after they have touched it. There is a good reason for this. Before the bits of paper touched the rod, they were *attracted* by the

Fountain Pen

Pipe Stem

Rubber Comb

Glass Rod

WILL PRODUCE STATIC ELECTRICITY

A number of common objects will produce static electricity when rubbed. A glass rod, a hard rubber or Lucite comb, a hard rubber pipe stem or a fountain pen made of plastic may be used in your experiments.

electricity on the rod. They themselves had no electrical charge—all the electricity was on the rod. They were neutral, as it is called. But when they came into contact with the rod, some of the electricity on the glass spread itself over the surface of the paper bits. The paper became covered with electricity or charged, as it is called. From this experiment it may be seen that there is no attraction between two substances when they are both charged, but that quite the contrary, they repel each other. When Thales performed this experiment he used a piece of amber instead of a glass rod of course, and instead of paper, little pieces of straw or lint.

ONE OF THE LAWS OF ELECTRICITY

No matter how many times you try this little experiment which has just been described, the same thing will always happen. Some of the little pieces of paper will first jump up to touch the rod and then fly off again. This is because electricity always obeys certain rules or laws, as they are called. Since there are a great many definite rules which govern the behavior of electricity and it always obeys them, it is what scientists call an exact science. One of the laws of electricity was discovered by means of the experiment which we have just been talking about. It is that when two objects become charged with the same kind of electricity they are no longer attracted to each other. In fact, they are repelled or pushed away. That is why some of the bits of paper fly away from the rod. They become charged with the same kind of electricity.

It was the discovery of definite facts like this about electricity which eventually made it possible to build all sorts of electrical instruments and machinery. Not this one particular law or fact, of course, but a whole mass of them. By learning a lot of facts about electricity, you will be able to understand it better.

You may be able to observe the workings of this important law of electricity and at the same time perform an interesting experiment, if, instead of bits of paper, you use some very small pieces of charcoal. A burnt match broken into small fragments will supply the charcoal. Put the pieces of charcoal on a piece of metal. The top of a baking powder or coffee can will do very nicely. Hold the electrified glass rod over them. They will jump up to meet the rod but as soon as they touch it, they will fly off again more quickly than the pieces of paper did. The pieces of charcoal have no charge before they touch the rod; they are neutral. Once they touch the rod, however, they are charged or electrified—with the same kind of electricity which appeared on the rod when you rubbed it, and so are no longer attracted but are pushed away.

Before you can understand how electricity will sometimes behave and why certain electrical devices are made as they are, it is necessary to know something about

CONDUCTORS AND INSULATORS

A list of all the vast number of electrical devices which have been developed during the past one hundred years would include thousands of contrivances varying in size from the little bulb for a pocket flashlight to a giant locomotive. Copper, brass, iron, steel, nickel, platinum, tungsten, glass, porcelain, paper, rubber, silk, cotton, and many other materials, each one carefully chosen for a particular reason are used in the manufacture of these things. Glass is used for one part and copper for another because electricity behaves differently when it comes into contact with these two different substances. It happens that glass is an *insulator* of electricity and copper is a *conductor*. There is a great deal of difference in the ability of different substances to conduct or insulate and that decides which material is the best to use for a particular purpose when building electrical devices.

One of the reasons why you can produce electricity quite easily by rubbing sealing wax, hard rubber, glass, resin, and rock crystal is because they do not carry or conduct it away when it is generated. If a piece of iron or copper is rubbed, the electricity passes into the hand of the person holding the metal and down into the earth as fast as it is produced because metals are *conductors* of electricity. Glass and rubber are non-conductors or *insulators*. Some substances are neither good conductors nor good insulators and they are usually called partial conductors. Here is a list of various substances arranged so as to come under their proper classification.

CONDUCTORS	PARTIAL CONDUCTORS	NON-CONDUCTORS OR INSULATORS
Silver	Cotton	Glass
Copper	Dry wood	Silk
Iron	Marble	Resin
All other metals	Stone	Quartz
Liquid acids	Paper	Oils
Liquid alkalis	Damp air	Wool
Chemical salts in solution		Shellac
Impure water		Hard rubber
Earth		Wax
		Mica
		Dry air
		Porcelain

Any substance which is wet is a conductor.

After you have looked over these lists it should be easy for you to understand why electricity is usually led from place to place on copper wires mounted on glass knobs or insulators and why wires are usually covered with rubber. The glass and porcelain knobs and the rubber covering on wires help to prevent the electricity from leaking away.

If you do not have much luck experimenting with static electricity in the summer time, you will now understand why. Remember that it is due to moisture in the air. Damp air is a partial conductor and conducts the electricity away as fast as you can produce it.

Now that you understand something about insulators and conductors, you will also know that when you have generated electricity by rubbing a glass rod or a fountain pen you should not lay it down or permit it to touch anything if you do not want it to lose its charge. The amount of electricity which you are playing with is very small—infinitesimal is the best word to describe it.

HOW STATIC ELECTRICITY MAY BE DETECTED

Some of the scientists who were experimenting with electricity one hundred and fifty years ago devised very sensitive instruments for detecting weak charges of static electricity. They called them *electroscopes*. There are several varieties of electroscopes. One of the simplest forms which the young experimenter can build for himself is the pith ball or feather electroscope. Pith is very light— that is the reason why it is used. If you live in the country you can cut a piece of pith out of the center of a dry elderberry stalk. City boys will have to use a small piece of cork or a feather. When the electroscope is finished it will consist of a tiny ball of pith (make the ball as small as the head of a pin) tied to a fine silk thread supported from a wire set in a cork in the top of a bottle. You can also use a tiny ball of cork or a piece of feather down in place of the elder pith. The electroscope will be more sensitive if you split a silk thread so as to obtain one of the fibers and use it to suspend the ball or feather.

Another electroscope which will respond to an almost unbelievably small amount of electricity can be made with a piece of gold leaf. Two narrow strips of the thinnest tissue paper may be used instead of gold leaf but will not be as sensitive. If you use tissue paper it should have a little dry bronze powder (the powder which is mixed with a liquid for painting radiators) rubbed on it before it is used. The strips are hung upon a wire and will repel one another and stand apart when touched with a charged fountain pen. The force of gravity which makes them hang down straight is overcome by the repelling force of the electrical charge. Gold leaf is very much better to use than tissue paper. You can obtain a sheet of gold leaf from a sign painter. They use it in lettering show windows and business signs. Gold leaf is so thin that it is almost impossible for an inexperienced person to handle it, and when you get your electroscope ready you had better ask the painter to hang the strips of gold leaf on for you. The two pieces of gold leaf should be about one-quarter of an inch wide and one inch long. They are suspended from a piece of copper wire bent into the shape of the letter "L." The wire passes through a cork fitting into the top of a wide-mouthed glass jar or bottle. The jar serves to protect the gold leaf from draughts of air and as an insulator. A sign painter will know how to attach the gold-leaf strips to the wire with a sticky liquid called "size." Then you can lower them carefully into the jar and put the cork in place. The top of the jar should be sealed by painting the cork with some melted paraffin. The upper end of the wire is bent so as to form a little circle. When kept dry and free from dust, this little instrument is very sensitive.

An electrified fountain pen or glass rod brought near a gold leaf electroscope will cause the leaves to repel one another even while two or three feet away. The wooden chips produced by sharpening a pencil over the electroscope so that they fall on the wire will be found to be electrified and cause the leaves to spread apart. Brushing the wire with a dry camel's-hair artist's brush is sometimes enough friction to produce electricity whose presence will be shown by movement of the gold leaves. The electricity on the leaves can be discharged at any time by touching the wire with the finger.

THE FIRST ELECTRICAL MACHINE

A little more than three hundred years ago, scientists were doing these same experiments which have just been described for you.

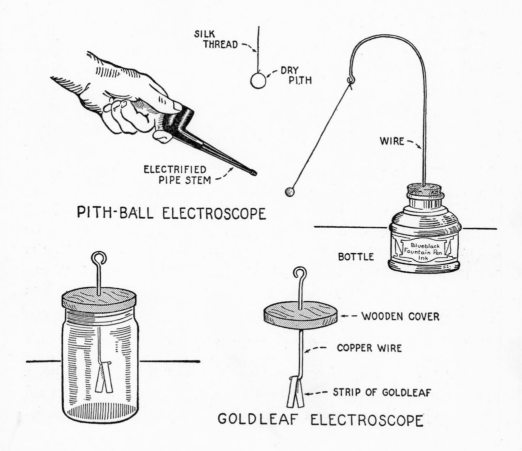

EXPERIMENTS WITH STATIC ELECTRICITY

Two simple forms of electroscope which will reveal the presence of static electricity.

SILK THREAD

DRY PITH

WIRE

ELECTRIFIED PIPE STEM

PITH-BALL ELECTROSCOPE

Blueblack Fountain Pen Ink

BOTTLE

WOODEN COVER

COPPER WIRE

STRIP OF GOLDLEAF

GOLDLEAF ELECTROSCOPE

They were producing electricity in infinitesimal quantities by rubbing all sorts of objects with silk and wool and fur and trying to attract small fragments of various substances. No one knew how to produce electricity any differently or anything else to do with it after it had been generated. There was no way known how to keep it or store it after it had been produced. It was just the same flighty stuff that you can produce on a fountain pen.

A LEYDEN
JAR

Whenever there is a new idea needed someone always comes along with it sooner or later. This time it was the German philosopher named Otto Von Guericke who was Burgomaster of Magdeburg for thirty-five years. Von Guericke spent his spare time experimenting with electricity and it was not long before he grew tired of rubbing objects by hand. So he made the first *machine* for generating electricity. He mounted a ball of sulfur on a wooden shaft and fitted it with a crank so that it could be turned. When a piece of fur was held against the revolving ball, it generated static electricity. Von Guericke's machine worked beautifully, and while it was really only a plaything because there was nothing to do with electricity in those days except to play with it, it was nevertheless an electrical generating machine. Someone had to build the first one if there was to be any progress. There had to be a starting point in the development of electrical machinery. The honor belongs to Burgomaster Von Guericke.

THE LEYDEN JAR

In 1745, not long after Von Guericke invented his machine, a man named Kleist discovered how to store electricity with the aid of a glass jar. A year later another scientist, named Van Musschenbroek, who lived in Leyden, Holland, made the same discovery and the new device was called the Leyden jar, which name is still used till this day. Kleist and Van Musschenbroek used water in the first jars which they built, but a famous Englishman found that it was much better to coat the inside and outside of the jar with tin-foil and omit the water. Electricity could now be stored up in large quantities in Leyden jars and sometimes kept for several days. Leyden jars were the first form of the device called an electrical "capacitor." Capacitors are an important part of telephones, radio transmitters and receivers, and other electrical apparatus. The invention of such a novel device as the Leyden jar, in those days caused scientists to take a fresh interest in electricity. When anything attracts the attention of a great many men, it is bound to make more progress than when only a few are interested. Actually, it took another one hundred and fifty years in order to make much progress in gathering the knowledge which finally enabled men to make telegraph instruments, telephones, electric locomotives, and radios, but it was Von Guericke's simple generating machine and the Leyden jar which started things moving in that direction.

CHAPTER TWO

ABOUT MAGNETISM

IF, as time went on, scientists and engineers had never been able to find any better method of generating electricity than by rubbing something, the great power plants which furnish current for electric lights, railways, and factories could never have been created. Telephone and telegraph systems and that great host of other familiar electrical devices would not exist. An oil lamp or a gas jet would still probably light our homes at night. There would be no radio receiver in the living room. We would have to be content with a phonograph.

But fortunately it so happened that playing and puttering with glass rods, magnets, wires, and chemicals taught experimenters two others ways of producing electricity. One of them was by making use of chemicals and the other way was with a magnet. It is the electricity generated by chemicals and magnets which we use for practical purposes. Magnets produce most of it for us—they produce the electricity generated in power houses. Magnets and magnetism are therefore of great importance, not only to the scientist and engineer but to all of us when we consider the benefits that they have brought.

THE FIRST MAGNETS

It is always interesting to know the history of anything. When we look into the history of the magnet, we find that it was at least

24

two thousand years ago that some unknown person first noticed that a black mineral called *lodestone* had the curious power of picking up small pieces of iron. Unlike the amber which would pick up small light objects, a lodestone did not need to be rubbed and—stranger still—it would not disturb dust, chaff, feathers, or any of the other things attracted by amber but only draw iron or other bits of lodestone. This is because the power of the lodestone lies in its magnetism and not in electricity as in the case of the amber.

THE FIRST MAGNET

The first magnet was a hard black mineral called lodestone. This one has been dipped in iron filings and the filings are clinging to the ends in tufts.

One of the most surprising things about a lodestone is its ability to give magnetism to steel. A piece of hardened steel itself becomes a magnet if it is rubbed on a lodestone. One of the most amazing things of all is the fact that a lodestone does not lose any of its own magnetism when it gives its ability to a piece of steel.

However, just as in the case of its yellow brother, amber, the black lodestone remained merely a curiosity for many centuries after it was discovered. It was not until about six hundred years ago that lodestone found a use. Then an unknown inventor whose name has been lost in the mists of time made a wonderful discovery. He rubbed a piece of steel with a lodestone so as to magnetize it and then attached a string to the center and hung it up. The piece of steel swung slowly back and forth for a minute and then came to rest pointing in a north and south position. If it was disturbed, it always came back to rest pointing in the same direction. Here at last was a way to tell direction. It was the first compass.

THE FIRST COMPASS

About the end of the thirteenth century mariners commenced to use the compass aboard their ships as a guide when the sun and stars were hidden by clouds. Just think! Up to that time, vessels hardly dared venture out of sight of shore for the very good reason that it was often difficult to find the way back. But now sailors could go forth into unknown seas and find new lands. A magnetic needle would guide them. They need never lose their sense of direction. The exploration of the earth's surface has been one of the greatest accomplishments of the human race. It was the compass which made it possible.

A POCKET COMPASS

A pocket compass is a simple affair. A magnetized needle shaped like an arrow swings over a scale divided into degrees and marked with the points of the compass.

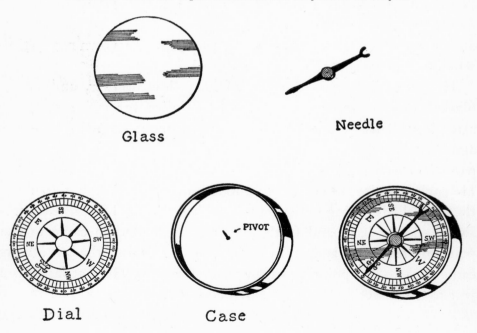

Glass   Needle

Dial   Case

The magnetic compass which surveyors and hunters use on land to tell direction is almost as simple as the first one which the unknown inventor made. It is nothing more than a flat steel needle which has been magnetized and supported on a pivot at its center. The needle swings over a scale divided into degrees and also marked with the "points" of the compass. The needle and its scale are enclosed in a small case with a glass crystal like a watch.

THE MARINER'S COMPASS

used by sailors and navigators to guide their ships when out of sight of land is constructed somewhat differently from the one used by surveyors and hunters but works in exactly the same way. It has three parts—called the *bowl*, the *card*, and the *needle*. The bowl is a brass cup, filled with alcohol and tightly sealed with a glass cover so that none of the alcohol can leak out. The card is a circular disk which floats in the alcohol.

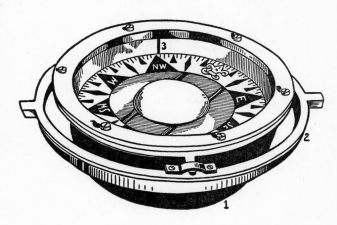

A MARINER'S COMPASS
1 is the bowl, 2 is one of the gimbals, and 3 is the lubber's line.

In the center of the card is a little socket which rests on an upright pin fixed in the bottom of the bowl so that the card can swing around on it. The magnetized needles—and there are generally two or more—are fastened to the bottom of the card. When the needles move, the card must move with them. The top of the card is marked around its edge with the 360 degrees of a circle and the thirty-two points of the compass. The four principal points or "cardinals," as they are called, are North, South, East and West. The other twenty-eight are the points in between. Naming the different compass points in their proper order, sailors call "boxing" the compass.

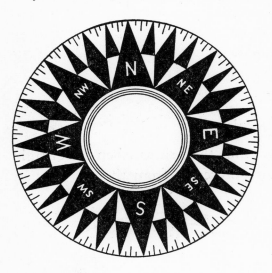

A COMPASS CARD

The bowl with its card and needles is mounted in a brass ring called a gimbal, so that it always remains in a horizontal position, even though the ship pitches and rolls considerably. The point on the compass card which is closest to a black mark on the bowl, called the "Lubber's line," shows the direction in which the ship is travelling.

ARTIFICIAL MAGNETS

For a long time, magnets were of no use for anything except building compasses—and the lodestone was of no use except for rubbing pieces of steel to form magnets for compasses. When it was found how to make some of the electrical instruments, such as telephones and meters, it was also found that magnets could be useful for other purposes besides building compasses and that there was a better way of making them than rubbing a piece of steel with a lodestone.

One of the nicest things about science is that everything seems to have just the right sort of a name. Pieces of steel which have been magnetized are called *artificial* magnets to distinguish them from the lodestone which is known as a *natural* magnet.

Artificial magnets are made in many forms so as to fit into some part of the electrical instrument for which they are made. The one with which everyone is usually the most familiar is the little toy "horseshoe" magnet. These are almost always painted red, but the red paint has nothing to do with magnetism. The little piece of soft iron which fits across the end of the horseshoe is called the *armature* or the "keeper" and it is intended to be always kept in place when the magnet is not in use be-

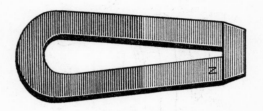

A HORSESHOE MAGNET

The experiments which may be performed with a magnet open the door to a scientific wonderland.

cause it actually helps the magnet to keep its magnetism. A magnet without its keeper will become weak after a while.

The horseshoe magnet itself is made of hardened steel but the little armature is soft iron. Hardened steel will retain its magnetism for many years, if it is treated properly, but soft iron loses it almost immediately. Steel will also lose its magnetism when it is heated or hammered. Dropping a magnet will weaken it. So, if you have a magnet, you must take proper care of it if you want it to keep its strength.

The ends of a magnet where you will find nearly all of its strength are called the *poles*. One pole may be marked with a straight line or the letter "N." This is called the "north" pole because if a horseshoe magnet could be straightened out and arranged to swing like a compass needle, it is this pole which would point towards the north. The other pole is the "south."

WHERE ARE PERMANENT MAGNETS USED?

If you look inside a telephone receiver, a telephone bell, a voltmeter or an ammeter, an electric light meter or a magneto you will find a permanent magnet. It will not be painted red. It will prob-

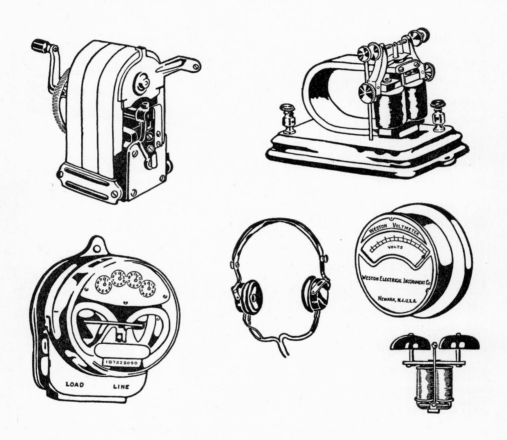

SOME ELECTRICAL INSTRUMENTS WHICH USE PERMANENT MAGNETS

A permanent magnet is a necessary part of each one of these electrical instruments. See if you can pick out the telephone magneto, polarized relay, electric light meter, voltmeter, telephone receiver and telephone bell.

ably be black and may not even be in the shape of a horseshoe but it nevertheless is an important part of these devices. They could not do their work without it.

HOW TO MAKE YOUR OWN MAGNETS

Making magnets is rather an easy matter if you already have a magnet. You can buy small horseshoe magnets at toy stores. Any piece of steel which has been hardened and tempered will become strongly magnetized if it is properly rubbed on one of the poles of another magnet. Sewing needles, knitting needles, crochet hooks, hacksaw blades, pieces of clock spring, drills, and the blades of knives and screw drivers are some of the things you can magnetize.

Try a large darning needle first and this will show you the trick of how to do the thing properly. Stroke the needle from the center towards one end (always in the same direction) with one pole of your horseshoe magnet. Then dip the needle in some iron filings and it will be found that the filings will cling to the needle in a tuft at each end. The needle has been magnetized—it has become a magnet. The ends where the filings cling are its poles. That is where the magnetism is strongest. If you had a piece of lodestone which you could dip into some iron filings, the same thing would happen. There would be two places where the filings would cling to the lodestone in a whiskerlike tuft—these would be the poles.

MAGNETIC FORCE

The pull of a magnet upon a piece of iron is not the same at all distances. You cannot feel it when the magnet is far away from the iron. The power with which a magnet attracts or pulls a piece

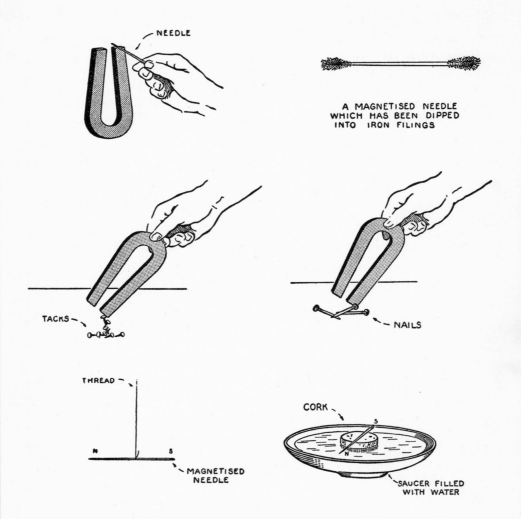

NEEDLE

A MAGNETISED NEEDLE
WHICH HAS BEEN DIPPED
INTO IRON FILINGS

TACKS

NAILS

THREAD

N   S

MAGNETISED
NEEDLE

CORK

SAUCER FILLED
WITH WATER

EXPERIMENTS WITH A MAGNET

The upper left-hand sketch shows how to magnetize a sewing needle by rubbing it across one pole of a horseshoe magnet. A magnetized needle which has been dipped in iron filings will gather tufts of the filings at the ends. A horseshoe magnet must be brought closer to iron nails than to iron tacks before it will lift them because the nails are heavier. A magnetized sewing needle swinging on a thread makes a simple compass. A magnetized needle laid on a cork floating in a saucer of water will also act as a compass.

of iron is called the *magnetic force* and it is much stronger when the magnet is near the iron. You can easily prove this if you place a carpet tack on the table and hold a magnet above it. Gradually lower the magnet until the tack jumps up to meet it. Notice how close the magnet is when the tack jumps. It did not jump at first because the magnetic force was not strong enough until the magnet was close to the tack. Next try a nail which is heavier than the tack. Notice that the magnet has to be brought much closer to the nail than it did to the tack before anything happens. The nail requires more magnetic force to lift it than the tack and so the magnet has to be moved down to where the force or pull is stronger. *The strongest magnetic force is always closest to the magnet.*

MAGNETISM

The mysterious power which you cannot see but which lifted the tack and nail and which is known as *magnetic force* by the electrical engineer is also called magnetism. Don't ask what it is because it is another one of those things which cannot be explained. Scientists offer an answer to the question but their answer is only at the best a guess and is apt to be changed almost any time. Magnetism is an enigma but it is a very useful mystery. It is the secret of almost all electrical machinery. It will do queer things—it will pass through most substances very easily. Your horseshoe magnet will attract a small nail or tack through a piece of paper, cloth, thin wood or glass just as if nothing intervened. It will also attract through brass, copper, aluminum and most of the metals. Through an iron plate, however, the magnetic force is much reduced or entirely stopped because the iron plate itself takes up the magnetism and prevents it from passing through and reaching the nail.

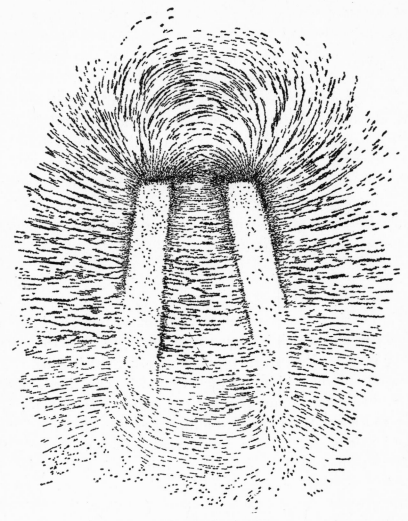

A MAGNETIC PHANTOM

The space in the neighborhood of a magnet is more interesting in many ways than the magnet itself. Iron filings sprinkled on a sheet of paper resting on a magnet will arrange themselves in a "phantom."

MAGNETIC SUBSTANCES

Try picking up small bits of paper, wood, brass, coal, glass, etc., with your magnet. You will not find anything which will be attracted except iron and steel because iron and steel are the only common substances which are magnetic. The metals called cobalt and nickel are slightly magnetic and are attracted, but not sufficiently so that you are apt to discover it with your litle horseshoe magnet.

In a laboratory equipped with sensitive instruments it can also be shown that *aluminum* and the rare metal called *platinum*, are slightly attracted by a powerful magnet while *bismuth*, *phosphorous*, *antimony*, and water are repelled or pushed away to a small extent.

WHAT IS IN THE SPACE AROUND A MAGNET?

The man who made the first dynamo, Michael Faraday was his name, was one of the world's greatest experimenters. It was because he was interested in magnetism that he discovered how to make a dynamo. He performed hundreds of experiments with magnetism and the more he wondered and thought about it, the more he suspected that the space in the neighborhood of a magnet might be as interesting as the magnet itself. Later this proved to be true, especially to the electrical engineer.

You can investigate the space around a magnet if you care to. Here is the way to do it. Lay a horseshoe magnet under a stiff piece of paper and then sprinkle some iron filings over the paper. Something curious will happen. Tap the paper gently so as to jar it slightly and the filings will arrange themselves in curved lines, spreading out from one pole of the magnet and curving around back to the opposite pole. Directly between the poles the lines of filings pass straight across. You have made what is called a magnetic "phantom" and the line of filings show that there is *something* in the space about a magnet. They show that something to be what is called lines of magnetic force. The phantom of a magnetic

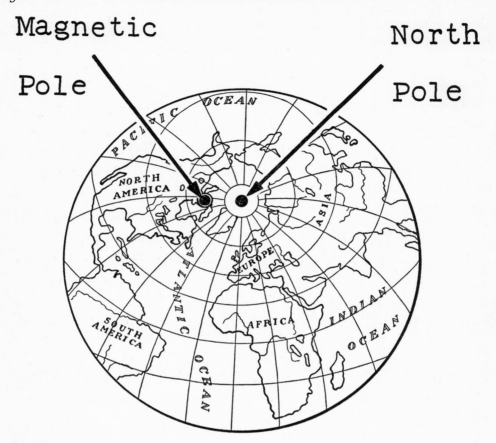

Magnetic Pole

North Pole

THE EARTH IS A MAGNET

needle or a bar magnet will be somewhat different in shape but will also show the pattern of the lines of magnetic force curving around through space about the magnet.

THE EARTH'S MAGNETISM

Did you know that you are living on a magnet? Well, you are. The big round ball upon which we live is a great whirling magnet.

Why this is so, no one knows. But the earth is magnetized and has a field of magnetic force about it just like a horseshoe or bar magnet—and all this immense amount of magnetism is practically going to waste because no way has ever been found to make use of it except in making a compass. If the earth was not magnetized there could not be any magnetic compasses. It is the earth's own field of magnetic force which pulls on the compass needle and turns it around so that it points north and south. If you bring a magnet near a compass you will find that you can pull the needle around in any direction that you wish without touching it. When you remove the magnet far enough away so that the needle is no longer under its influence, the needle will swing back to its usual north and south position and come to rest. It is the earth's magnetic force which is at work again pulling it around.

The earth itself has poles just like a magnet and by this we do not mean the usual north and south poles but rather two points on the earth's surface where the magnetism is the strongest.

We speak of the compass needle as pointing north and south but this is not entirely accurate for there are only a few places on the earth where a compass does point exactly north and south. This is because the magnetic poles of the earth are not in the same place as the geographical poles. In New York City the compass points about eleven degrees away from true north.

The angle formed between a line drawn from a magnetic compass to the geographic north pole (true north) and a line from the compass to the magnetic north pole (magnetic north) is called the compass variation. As previously mentioned, the compass variation is different for every geographical location. Surveyors and navigators using a magnetic compass in their work employ maps and charts which show the variation at their locality and can calculate accordingly. Gyroscopic compasses now used on ships and airplanes are not influenced by the earth's magnetic poles and point to true or geographical north.

HOW TO MAKE A COMPASS

A simple compass is easy to make. If you magnetize a darning needle and then hang it up with a long thread tied to its center so that it will balance, the needle will swing around and finally come to rest pointing in a north and south position.

A large needle which has been magnetized and laid on a flat cork floating in a basin of water will become a compass. The end of the needle which points north is called the *north seeking pole* and the opposite end is called the *south seeking pole*. These names are usually abbreviated to the more simple terms "north" and "south." It is the north pole of a horseshoe or bar magnet which seeks to turn towards the north and is marked with the letter "N" or with a line.

PERMANENT MAGNETS

All magnets may be divided into two classes, that is, *permanent* magnets and *electromagnets*.

A permanent magnet is one which, like the lodestone, retains a nearly constant magnetic power for an indefinite period. The permanent magnets used in the electrical industry are made of a hardened steel alloy and are magnetized by placing them in a strong magnetic field. Until this page, only permanent magnets have been described in this book. An electromagnet or *temporary* magnet is one in which the magnetic field is produced by an electric current. Electromagnets and electromagnetism are fully explained in Chapter Four.

ALNICO MAGNETS

Until about 1910, carbon steel with a relatively low melting point (called *eutectoid* carbon steel) was the only material available for making satisfactory permanent magnets. Today there are two general groups of materials used to manufacture permanent magnets— the so-called older steels and the newer alloys. The term "older steels" includes carbon steel, chromium steel, tungsten steel and cobalt steel. Carbon steel is still used to make some toys and cheap compasses. Chromium, tungsten and cobalt steels are in general use in the manufacture of permanent magnets but are being rapidly displaced by nickel-aluminum-iron alloys known in this country as Alnico. Many variations of this basic composition are used. They possess a greater amount of magnetic energy than any of the older materials. In other words, they make it practical to produce "stronger magnets of smaller size." Another quality of the Alnico materials is that Alnico powders can be pressed and sintered. Powdered Alnico can be pressed in a die to a desired shape and then baked at high temperature or sintered, as it is called, until it becomes hard. Small permanent magnets of complicated shape which are exceedingly difficult to cast or machine can be produced efficiently from Alnico powders by pressing and sintering and require little or no finishing. An Alnico magnet can be magnetized so that it has more than two poles and the poles are not necessarily at the ends.

ALNICO PERMANENT MAGNETS MADE BY THE SINTERING PROCESS

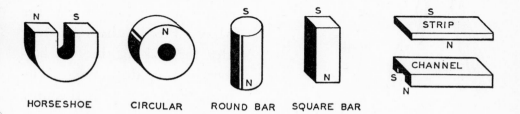

HORSESHOE   CIRCULAR   ROUND BAR   SQUARE BAR

CHAPTER THREE

ABOUT BATTERIES

THE picture of a pair of frog's legs which you will find on this page probably appears in more electrical books than any other illustration. You will immediately wonder what a frog's legs may have to do with electricity and why they are so important. But it is often just such an apparently trivial thing as this, something for which there does not seem to be any particular useful purpose that develops into a valuable new invention of use to all humanity. It was a teakettle which gave James Watt the idea which he developed into the first steam engine and it is said that the Montgolfier brothers got their idea for making the first balloon by watching smoke go up the chimney. It was the hind legs of a dead frog which revealed the secret of how to make the first electric battery.

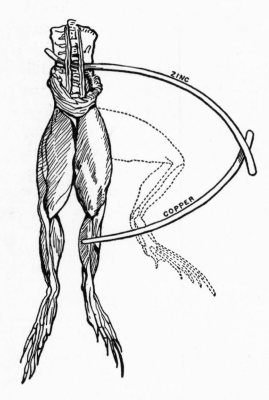

GALVANI'S FAMOUS DISCOVERY

A pair of frog's legs may seem out of place in a book about electricity but it was the hind legs of a dead frog that gave the clue to the first battery.

40

When you take the old battery out of your flashlight and put in a new one, you probably do it as a matter of course and are more interested at the time in finding out how bright the lamp will burn with the new battery than anything else. But for a moment you have had something in your hands which was one of the most important scientific discoveries ever made—the discovery that *electricity could be produced with chemicals*—a steady *current* of electricity which would last for hours—far different from a restless static charge ready to be gone in a jiffy. It gave scientists a form of electricity which would stay around long enough so that they could get acquainted with it. They could now perform countless new experiments.

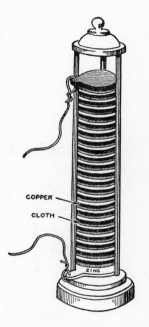

COPPER

CLOTH

ZINC

VOLTA'S PILE

Volta's pile was the first electric battery. It consisted of alternate disks of copper and zinc arranged in a pile.

THE FIRST BATTERY

The discovery made two men famous. One of these, Luigi Galvani, was a professor of anatomy in the University of Bologna, Italy. Anatomy is the science of the structure of the bodies of human beings and animals. Anatomists cut up dead bodies to study and experiment with. One day in 1780 when Professor Luigi Galvani was puttering around in his laboratory with the hind legs of some dead frogs, he was very much startled by a strange happening. The dead frog's legs twitched and kicked several times as if they were alive. Galvani set about finding the cause of their unusual behavior and discovered that if a piece of metal was touched to the nerves in the frog's backbone and a different metal laid against

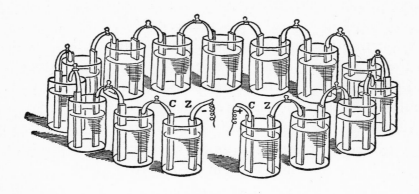

VOLTA'S "CROWN OF CUPS"

the leg muscles, the dead legs would jump and kick whenever the two metals were touched together. He found that he always had to use two different metals. Just think what a surprising discovery it must have been to find a way to cause something dead to move as if it were alive. Galvani of course wanted an explanation and he decided that the nerves of the dead frog generated what he called a "vital fluid" and that when he provided a metal pathway for the invisible "fluid" to flow between the backbone and the leg muscles, the legs would kick and twitch. He did not know that he had really discovered the very important fact that electricity could be produced in other ways than by friction and that the electricity thus produced was a *current* and not a *static charge*. He published a scientific paper in 1791 telling about his experiments and the reason he believed the frog's legs moved.

Most great discoveries have been made step by step. One man could not do it all. Someone else, using the knowledge of the first man, has taken up the work and made still further discoveries. This is exactly what happened in the case of the frog's legs. At the time Galvani published the story of his experiments there was at the University of Pavia, about 125 miles northwest of Bologna, a professor of physics by the name of Alessandro Volta. Now a professor of physics is not so much interested in nerves and muscles as he is in metals. Volta repeated Galvani's experiments and was very much struck by the fact that two different metals were necessary in order to make a dead frog's legs kick. He decided that there was no mysterious "vital fluid" in the dead frog's nerves and muscles but that *electricity* was produced when two different metals touched each other. It was electricity which made the frog's legs move.

THE VOLTAIC PILE

He proved his belief by constructing what is called a Voltaic pile. He found that by arranging several pairs of metals he could

SIZE makes no difference in VOLTAGE

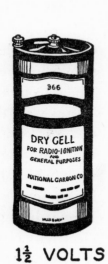

DRY CELL
FOR RADIO-IGNITION
AND
GENERAL PURPOSES

NATIONAL CARBON CO

1½ VOLTS

UNIT CELL
FOR FLASHLIGHTS
NATIONAL CARBON

1½ VOLTS

VOLTAGE

Each of these cells, although different in size, delivers the same voltage or electrical pressure. The larger cell gives the most amperage or volume of current.

build up the small amount of electricity generated in each pair into quite a strong current. He made the "pile" by placing a pair of zinc and copper disks in contact with one another, then laying on the copper disk a piece of flannel soaked in brine, then on top of this another pair of metal disks and so on until several pairs were stacked up. By connecting a wire to the last copper and the first zinc disk considerable current was produced.

THE VOLTAIC CELL

Volta soon improved his first idea by changing the pile into what he called a *Couronne de Tasse*, which means a "crown of cups" in French. To do this, he filled a number of cups with salt water or dilute acid and placed a strip of copper and a strip of zinc in each cup. The copper strip in each cup was connected to the zinc strip in the next cup just as you would connect a number of dry cells together. A much more powerful electric current could be obtained

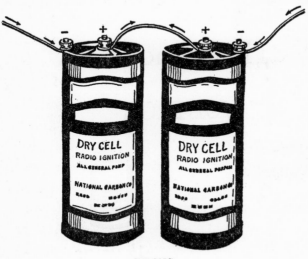

WRONG

The wrong way to connect two dry cells in series. The connecting wire should join the zinc of one cell to the carbon of the other as shown in the next illustration.

between the last zinc and copper of the Couronne de Tasse than from the "pile." The Couronne de Tasse was the *first real battery*. It was the starting point from which has been built our present knowledge of how electricity can be useful. Volta revealed his discovery to the world in 1800 by publishing an account of his experiments. Since then, other experimenters have made many different forms of batteries, most of them much more powerful than those which Volta built. But every one of them still retains the principle of Volta's cups in that there must be two different metals or *elements* and a liquid or *electrolyte*. The zinc and copper strips were the elements of Volta's battery and the dilute sulphuric acid the electrolyte.

Some of the boys who read this book may be curious and want to ask

HOW DOES A BATTERY MAKE ELECTRICITY?

If you ask the question just that way the answer will have to be, "a battery does not make electricity." But if instead you should

say, "but where does the electricity come from?" you can have a more satisfactory answer right away. The electricity is in the chemicals, in the sulfuric acid, in the water and the zinc. It is imprisoned there and cannot get out until these substances come together and chemical action starts. According to modern scien-

RIGHT

The right way to connect two dry cells in series.

tific theory, energy is either liberated or absorbed in all chemical reactions. The chemical activity in Voltaic cells releases energy in the form of heat and electricity. The heat escapes into the atmosphere. The electricity flows out of a cell when a conducting pathway is connected to its elements.

Before a vast network of power wires was stretched all over this country, batteries were used for many purposes for which an electric power system now supplies electric current. Railway signals, telephones, telegraphs, small motors, and many other electrical devices once depended upon Voltaic batteries of some sort. In some places they still do—for batteries are still used in laboratories but the only sort that the average boy is apt to see today are the dry types used to ring doorbells, to operate flashlights, portable radios, hearing aids, etc.

A DRY CELL IS NOT REALLY DRY

If it were, it would not work. It is moist inside. If you break open an old flashlight cell you will find a zinc cup which has been filled with powdered chemicals packed around a carbon rod. The zinc is the zinc element which Volta used but his copper strip has been replaced by the carbon rod. The carbon rod is usually enclosed in a little cloth bag packed with a black mixture which consists of powdered carbon and a chemical called manganese dioxide. Volta's original batteries tired very quickly when they were used. The electric current which they gave forth was stronger at first than it was a half hour later. This tiring is called *polarization* and is due to tiny bubbles of hydrogen gas which form on the carbon. A way was found to avoid this. Manganese dioxide is a chemical which has the ability to absorb hydrogen and so some of it is mixed with carbon and packed around the carbon rod to prevent the dry cell from tiring or becoming *polarized* quickly. The carbon rod and its surrounding packing are moistened with a solution of zinc chloride and sal ammoniac. This liquid is the electrolyte which corresponds to the dilute acid which Volta used. The white material which you will find next to the zinc

Wax Seal

Terminal

Powdered Carbon
and Manganese

Carbon Rod

Paper Cup

SPECIAL N°6
DRY CELL

FOR RADIO
AND
GENERAL PURPOSES

SPECIAL N°6
DRY CELL

FOR RADIO
AND
GENERAL PURPOSES

Zinc Cup

Paper Case

A NO. 6 DRY CELL

If you take a dry cell apart you will find it is made of the parts shown in this sketch.
No. 6 indicates the size, namely 6 inches high by 2½ inches in diameter.

cup is a chemical paste made of zinc chloride, sal ammoniac and
wheat flour. The top of the cell is sealed with a black wax to prevent the contents from spilling out or evaporating.

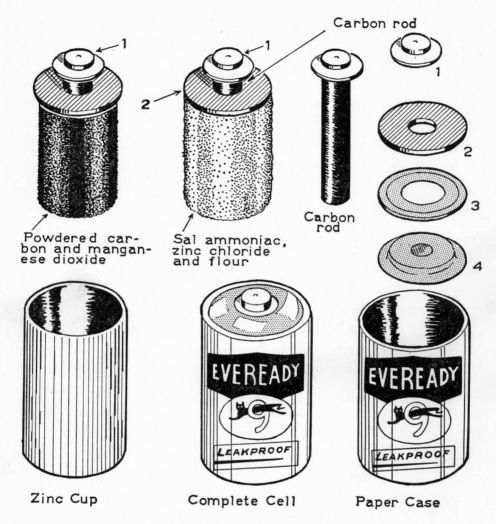

Carbon rod

1

2

Carbon rod

1

2

3

4

Powdered carbon and manganese dioxide

Sal ammoniac, zinc chloride and flour

Zinc Cup   Complete Cell   Paper Case

ZINC–CARBON–SAL AMMONIAC FLASHLIGHT CELL
Brass contact (1), paper washer (2), metal top (3), steel bottom (4).

Larger dry cells are made on the same plan as the small ones used in flashlights except that a blotting paper cup is used to replace the cloth bag. Dry cells are well adapted to furnish small currents for long periods or moderate currents intermittently. They are not suit-able for furnishing large currents. A few years ago most batteries were comparatively expensive. Nowadays they are quite cheap. You can buy dry cells for less than it would cost you to purchase the mate-rials of which they are made. There are four standard sizes of dry cells for flashlights manufactured in the United States of America.

When speaking of cells and batteries do not make the common mistake of referring to a single cell as a "battery" but call it a "cell." A battery is a group of two or more cells.

HOW TO MAKE A BATTERY

It would be easy to make a battery of cells just like Volta's Couronne de Tasse, but the sulfuric acid which makes the best electrolyte is even when diluted dangerous stuff to get on your hands or clothing. It eats holes in many things. If you want to make an electric cell or a battery of them to experiment with, it would be better to make the type invented by a Frenchman named Leclanché. For this, you will need a strip of sheet zinc, a glass jar, a carbon rod and a chemical called sal ammoniac. The carbon rod may be ob-tained without any more expense than the little time required to break open an old dry cell with a chisel and a hammer. It is neces-sary to perform this operation carefully in order not to break the carbon. It should not be necessary to spend money for a glass jar. A pint-size fruit or mayonnaise jar will be suitable. Sal ammoniac is a white powder. Another name for the same substance is ammonium chloride. You can buy it at a hardware store, electrical shop or drug store. You will need about two ounces for each pint size cell. Each cell should have a wooden cover about three inches square and one-half of an inch thick. Cut a slot with a jigsaw blade so that the zinc strip will slip through the cover. Make a hole for the carbon rod which is a tight fit. The zinc strip should be about seven inches long

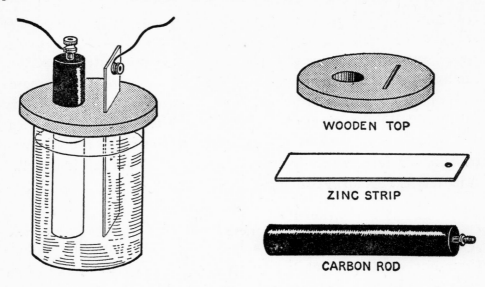

WOODEN TOP

ZINC STRIP

CARBON ROD

AN EXPERIMENTAL LECLANCHE CELL

and one inch wide. You should be able to buy heavy sheet zinc at a plumbing shop. It is a soft metal and you can cut it easily with a pair of snips.

To mix the electrolyte it is simply necessary to put about two ounces of sal ammoniac in the jar and pour one and one-half cups of water over it. Stir it with a clean stick until it dissolves.

When the zinc and carbon rod are slipped in place in the cover and immersed in the solution the battery is ready to go to work. You can use it for some of the experiments which are described later on in this book.

Dry cells are still used to ring doorbells, operate flashlights and electrical instruments which must be carried about, but that is about all that Voltaic batteries are used for nowadays except in a few out-of-the-way places where electricity cannot be obtained from the power wires. Railroads occasionally still use batteries for telegraphing, operating railroad crossing bells and signals. These are usually of the type called Edison or copper-oxide-zinc batteries. They are also used for police and fire alarm signals.

ZINC-MANGANESE DIOXIDE AND ZINC-MERCURIC OXIDE CELLS

Until a few years ago the zinc-carbon-sal ammoniac cell was the only type manufactured commercially. Now two new varieties are rapidly assuming an important place in the commercial dry cell industry, namely, the zinc-manganese dioxide cell and the zinc-mercuric oxide cell.

The zinc-manganese dioxide cell is also commonly known as an alkaline cell. It has a zinc negative element and a manganese dioxide positive element. The electrolyte is a solution of potassium hydroxide held in an absorbent material so that the cell is moist inside but contains no free liquid. A zinc-manganese dioxide cell will deliver 1.5 volts at its terminals. Its voltage is the same as that of a zinc-carbon-sal ammoniac cell but it will deliver a strong current (more amperage) with greater efficiency and for a longer time.

The zinc-mercuric oxide cell, popularly known as a mercury cell, has more energy-producing capacity per unit of volume and weight than the zinc-carbon-sal ammoniac cell. The negative element is a zinc-mercury amalgam,[1] separated from the positive element by an absorbent pad saturated with a solution of potassium hydroxide. The potassium hydroxide solution is the electrolyte. The positive element is a mixture of red mercuric oxide and graphite. The mercuric oxide also acts as a depolarizer. The cap or top teminal of a mercury cell is negative, the reverse of that of the zinc-carbon-sal ammoniac cell.

[1] An amalgam is an alloy of mercury with another metal.

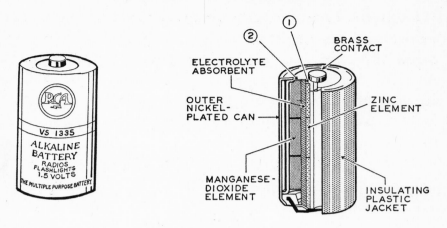

ZINC-MANGANESE OR ALKALINE DRY CELL

Mercury cells have a lower voltage (1.4 volts) than zinc-carbon-sal ammoniac and zinc-manganese dioxide cells.

THE EDISON CELL

One element in an Edison cell is a plate of copper oxide. The other is zinc. These are supported from a porcelain cover, resting on the top of a jar filled with a solution of caustic soda.

B BATTERIES FOR RADIO RECEIVERS

The 9-, 22½-, 45- and 90-volt batteries used in portable radios appear from the outside to be a single cell. Actually, they consist of a number of small dry cells connected in series and enclosed in a rectangular cardboard casing. There are thirty cells in a 45-volt B battery. The cells may be the conventional round type of construction used in making flashlight cells and be connected together by short wires. Or, they may be a flat form called "Layer-Bilt."

Layer-Bilt batteries bear resemblance to a Voltaic pile. Each cell consists of a flat carbon plate and a flat zinc plate with a sheet of porous paper between. The paper is saturated with sal ammoniac. An elastic rubber band around each cell forms a casing. The cells are piled up so that the carbon plate of one cell makes contact with the zinc plate of the next cell. There are no connecting wires between adjacent cells.

B BATTERIES

The B batteries used in portable radio receivers consist of a number of small dry cells connected in series and sealed in a cardboard box. The cells may be either cylindrical or flat. There is space between cylindrical cells which is wasted. In order to utilize this space and make B batteries as compact as possible, flat cells called Layer-Bilt are manufactured.

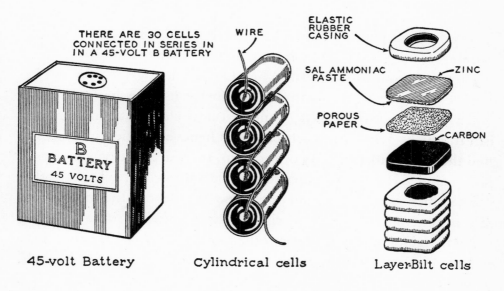

45-volt Battery　　　Cylindrical cells　　　Layer-Bilt cells

CHAPTER FOUR

HOW ELECTRICITY PRODUCES MAGNETISM

SOME of the great rivers of the world, so broad and deep that the largest ocean steamers can find in them a safe harbor, have their beginnings in the trickle of a tiny spring. The tall pine tree grows from one of the smallest of seeds. You can hold several thousand pine seeds in your hand. Like a tree or river, great developments in science sometimes come from the very smallest beginnings.

A tiny "scientific seed" which grew into several huge electrical enterprises was planted nearly one hundred and fifty years ago when a young Danish boy named Hans Christian Oersted decided that he wanted to become a scientist. When Oersted had grown up and become a professor of physics in the University at Copenhagen, he, like other scientists of those days, wondered how electricity and magnetism might be related to each other. Whenever a scientist wants to find the answer to a mystery or problem, there are three good ways of proceeding. He can ask someone who does know or read what other learned men may have found out and written about the matter. But at that time no one knew the right answer or had written anything very satisfactory to Oersted about the relationship between electricity and magnetism. So he decided to experiment and find out himself. That is the third way of getting an answer and sometimes the best.

Now an experiment is not a conjuring trick done for the sake of amusement but is a question asked of Nature in hopes of getting an answer. Nature is always ready to give a correct answer provided the question is properly asked by arranging the right experiment.

Oersted was a very busy experimenter and one day when he was getting his wires and batteries ready to try something new he accidentally found that when the current from one of the batteries flowed through a wire something surprising happened. When the wire was brought near a compass needle, the compass needle moved just as it did when a magnet was brought near it. The movement of a compass needle is really a small thing in itself but it may have a very big meaning, and that was exactly the case in Oersted's experiment. The slight movement of the compass needle which he mentioned meant that he had found out something which no one had ever known before. He had discovered that a *wire carrying a current of electricity produces magnetism.* It was this magnetism which moved his compass needle. Now that someone had

JOSEPH HENRY
He made one of the first electromagnets.

found out how to produce magnetism you may be sure that other experimenters would soon find out something useful to do with it. They did.

Not long after Oersted made his discovery, William Sturgeon found that when a coil of wire is wrapped around an iron bar, the iron will become a magnet whenever an electric current flows through the coil. Such an arrangement is called an *electromagnet.* Most of the electrical devices which are familiar things to us depend upon two things which electricity can do.

1. Generate heat.
2. Produce magnetism.

Electrical machines which move in any way depend upon electromagnetism. Telephone and telegraph instruments, motors, railway signals, horns and electric bells all contain one or more electromagnets.

Joseph Henry, an American scientist, who was born in Albany, New York, in 1797, made one of the first electromagnets. He was the first secretary of the Smithsonian Institution, and his magnet, which was said to be powerful enough to lift a blacksmith's anvil, is still in the museum.

It is an easy matter to repeat the experiments with which these scientists of a hundred years ago discovered some of the most valuable things we know about electricity.

ELECTRICITY CREATES MAGNETISM

If you have a compass, a small pocket compass, or even a homemade one will do, you can repeat Oersted's experiment. Connect one end of a wire to a dry cell and then bring the wire close to the compass needle. The wire should be parallel to the needle and about one inch above it. Nothing will happen until you make the circuit complete so that a current can flow, but when you touch the other end of the wire to the battery the needle will swing around at right angles.

HOW TO MAKE A GALVANOSCOPE

A very useful little device which you can use to detect feeble currents of electricity is called the galvanoscope. You can make one by wrapping forty or fifty turns of fine insulated copper wire around a pocket compass. Any size of wire ranging from No. 25 to No. 36 B. & S. gauge will be satisfactory. The compass may be set in the

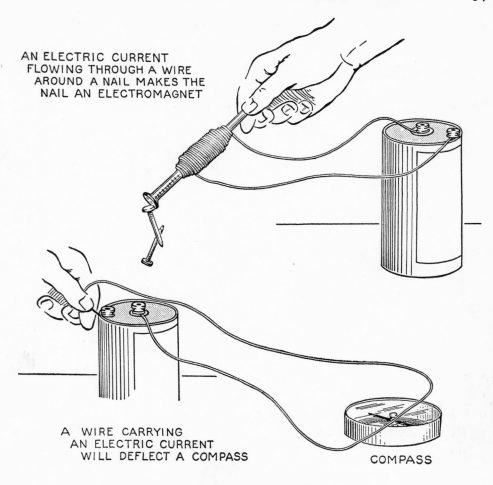

AN ELECTRIC CURRENT
FLOWING THROUGH A WIRE
AROUND A NAIL MAKES THE
NAIL AN ELECTROMAGNET

A WIRE CARRYING
AN ELECTRIC CURRENT
WILL DEFLECT A COMPASS

COMPASS

EXPERIMENTS WITH ELECTROMAGNETISM

Knowledge gained from these two simple experiments was put to practical use in making
the first telegraph and telephone instruments, motors, etc.

center of a small block of wood and the wire wrapped around both
the block and the compass, if you wish to make an instrument you
can keep. The wires should be bunched together as closely as possible and pass over the center of the needle. Attach the ends of the

wires to two binding posts mounted on the wooden block. You can make your own binding posts by using the knurled thumb nuts from an old dry cell. You will also need two brass screws and two hexagonal ("hex") nuts. You can buy these at almost any garage or hardware store. The thread on a battery nut is a size called 8–32.

ALESSANDRO VOLTA
He made the first battery.

The machine screw and the nut should also have an 8–32 thread so that they will all fit together.

Bore a hole through the wooden block for each binding post. An 8–32 machine screw is five thirty-seconds of an inch in diameter. A No. 19 drill will make the right size of hole for the screw to slip through.

The head of the screw should be on the underside of the wooden block. Put the "hex" nut on top. Before you tighten the nut, scrape the insulation off one end of the wire and wrap it around the screw so that when the nut is tightened the wire will be squeezed between the head of the screw and the wooden block. This will make a good electrical connection or contact between the screw and the wire.

The galvanoscope should be set on a table and turned so that the compass needle is parallel to the turns of wire forming the coil. A very feeble current of electricity passing through the coil will tend to swing the needle around at right angles.

Another way of making a very simple compass galvanoscope is by winding about fifty turns of fine insulated wire, No. 30–36 B. & S. gauge around the bottom of a glass tumbler so as to form a coil. Slip the coil from the glass and tie it in two or three places with a silk thread so that it will not come apart. Separate the strands of wire at one side slightly so that they are divided into two groups. Fasten the coil to the center of a wooden block with some sealing wax.

The compass needle for your galvanoscope should be a large sewing needle which has been carefully magnetized by rubbing it on a permanent magnet. The needle should be mounted in a little strip of heavy writing paper or drawing paper. Find the place at which the needle will balance in the paper strip and fasten it there with a small drop of hot sealing wax. A small hole is punched in the top of the paper strip through which to pass and tie a fine silk thread. The other end of the thread is supported by two wooden strips fastened together in the shape of the letter "L" and attached to the side of

EXPERIMENTS WITH AN ELECTRIC CURRENT

Two easily constructed galvanometers which will detect feeble currents of electricity.

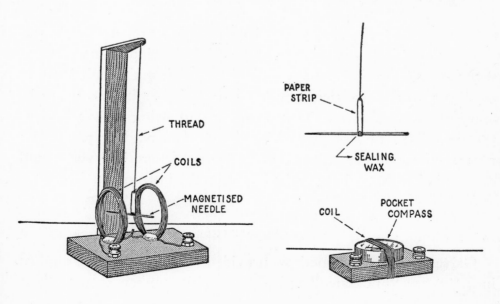

the wooden block or base. The thread should be fastened directly over the center of the coil. The paper strip and its needle swing in the center of the coil. The terminals of the coil are connected to two binding posts mounted on the base. When you use the galvanoscope it will be necessary to move it around until the wires in the coil are parallel to the needle after the needle has come to rest in a north and south position. A very feeble current of electricity flowing through the coil will cause the needle to swing around.

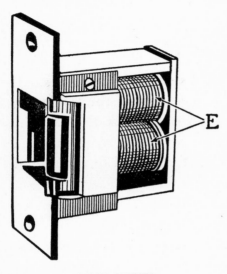

DOOR OPENER
A useful device which is operated by electromagnets (E).

Just as an electroscope is an instrument for detecting tiny charges of static electricity so the galvanoscope is used for detecting currents of electricity. It is a device that was much used by some of the first electrical experimenters. It was eventually developed into an instrument called a galvanometer, which would detect an unbelievably small current of electricity. Some of those in use in scientific laboratories are so sensitive that the needle will swing violently when the tips of the fingers are touched to the two binding posts. The contact of the fingers with the metal posts generates a very small current indeed but it is enough to show on the instrument.

GALVANOMETERS

Galvanoscopes are sometimes provided with a paper scale marked in degrees or "graduated" and marked with numbers so as to show

how far the needle moves. Such galvanoscopes are called *galvanometers*.

Galvanometers can be built so as to show the strength of an electrical current. They then become electrical measuring instruments called *voltmeters* and *ammeters*.

A PIECE OF WIRE AND A NAIL
BECOME AN ELECTROMAGNET

It is not difficult to make an electromagnet. You can make one in few minutes without much trouble looking for materials. If you wrap some insulated wire around an ordinary nail and connect it to a battery, you will have made an electromagnet which will pick up pieces of iron and steel. Iron filings, small nails and tacks will be attracted to the nail. If the nail is soft steel or iron, the magnetism will disappear as soon as the current ceases to flow through the coil.

But if the wire is wrapped around a piece of hardened or tempered steel, the steel will remain a magnet even after the current has ceased. It has become permanently magnetized. You can prove this by wrapping some wire around a screw driver blade, or a drill or chisel. It is in this way that the permanent magnets used in telephone bells, magnetos, telephone receivers, etc., are magnetized—by electricity—not by rubbing them on a magnet or a lodestone.

The electromagnets used on a great many electrical instruments are made by winding the wire on a "spool" or bobbin, having a round "core" of soft iron and two fibre ends to keep the wire from slipping off.

HORSESHOE ELECTROMAGNETS

When two electromagnets are mounted on a small iron bar called a "yoke" and properly connected together they form a "horseshoe" electromagnet and are much stronger than a single magnet.

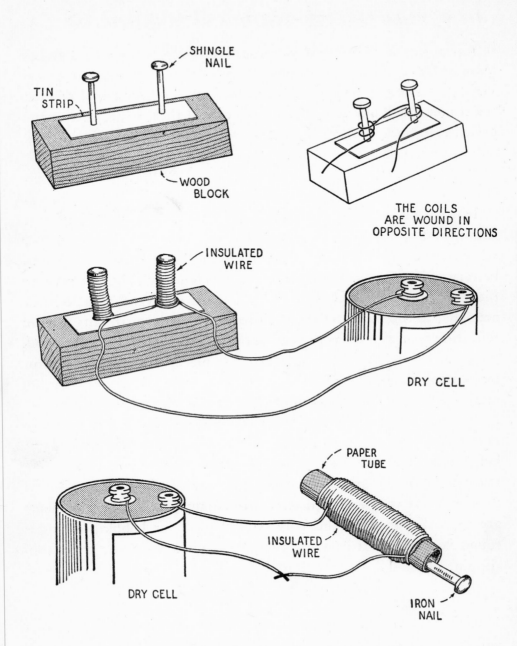

SHINGLE NAIL

TIN STRIP

WOOD BLOCK

THE COILS
ARE WOUND IN
OPPOSITE DIRECTIONS

INSULATED WIRE

DRY CELL

PAPER TUBE

INSULATED WIRE

DRY CELL

IRON NAIL

EXPERIMENTS WITH ELECTROMAGNETISM
The sketches show how to make a simple horseshoe electromagnet and a solenoid coil.

If you build a horseshoe electromagnet you can use it to do the same sort of experiments for which you might use a horseshoe permanent magnet. You will be surprised at its lifting power when connected to one or two cells of dry battery.

You can make a small horseshoe electromagnet with two shingle nails and a piece of tin. Lay a strip of tin on a small block of wood and drive a shingle nail through it into the wood. Do not drive the nail all the way but leave about five-eighths of an inch sticking out. Drive another nail about three-quarters of an inch away in the same manner. Wrap a strip of thin paper around each nail between the head and the tin. This is to insulate the nail from the wire and prevent a "short circuit." Wrap about fifty turns of fine insulated wire (Nos. 25 to 30 B. & S. gauge) around one nail and then without cutting the wire wrap the same number of turns around the other nail, taking care to wind the second coil in the *opposite* direction from the first. Tie the outside end of the wire so that it will not unwrap.

If you connect your electromagnet to a dry cell, you will be surprised at the amount of magnetism it will develop. If you hold the blade of a screw driver just above the poles (the nail heads have become the poles) of the magnets it will be pulled down with a jerk.

Lay a piece of cardboard on the poles and sprinkle some iron filings on the cardboard. Then see what happens when you connect the magnets to the battery. It will make a magnetic phantom something like that produced by the poles of a permanent magnet.

SOLENOIDS

Electrical engineers often use another type of electromagnet called a solenoid in building electrical machinery. You can make a solenoid by winding some wire around a small glass or paper tube.

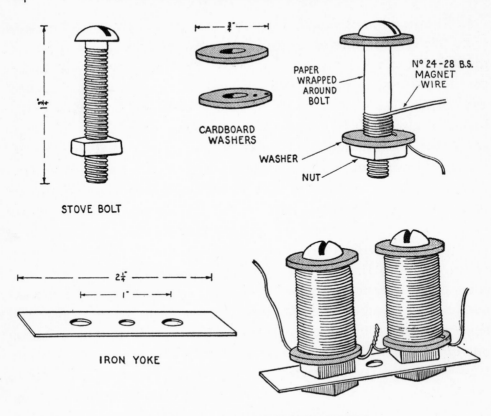

STOVE BOLT

CARDBOARD WASHERS

PAPER WRAPPED AROUND BOLT

N° 24-28 B.S. MAGNET WIRE

WASHER

NUT

IRON YOKE

EXPERIMENTS WITH ELECTROMAGNETISM

A horseshoe electromagnet built out of stove bolts, cardboard, tin, and wire will lift a surprisingly heavy weight.

If you stick the end of an iron nail in the end of the tube and connect the solenoid to a battery, the nail will be drawn inside the tube.

MAKING A HORSESHOE ELECTROMAGNET

A larger horseshoe magnet than the one made from the shingle nails and the strip of tin will be useful for many interesting experiments. You can use it to make a telegraph sounder, or a buzzer.

The core of each magnet should be a round-headed stove bolt one-quarter of an inch in diameter and one and three-quarter inches long. It is a good idea to heat the bolts red hot in a fire or the flame of a gas stove and let them cool off slowly so as to soften or "anneal" the metal. This is done so that the iron will not retain any magnetism after the current has ceased to flow through the coil. Two thick cardboard washers, three-quarters of an inch in diameter, are fitted on each core. If the washers are cut out and soaked in shellac they will be strong and stiff after the shellac has dried. One washer is placed snugly against the underside of the head of each bolt and the other about an inch below it. That portion of the bolt which is between the two washers is covered with two or three layers of writing paper so that when the wire is wound on, it cannot come into contact with the metal at any point. If you use plenty of shellac to cement the paper and washers in place and a nut against the underside of the lower washer, they will not slip while the wire is being wound in place. You will need to make two holes in the bottom washer to pass the terminals or ends of the wire through. The best way to make the holes is to burn them through with a red hot needle. One hole should be close to the core and the other near the outer edge of the washer.

Each magnet spool should be wound almost full of No. 24–28 B. & S. gauge insulated magnet wire using every care to wind on each layer smoothly and evenly. Slip the inside end of the wire through the hole in the washer next to the core. The outside end should be passed through the other hole. Wind the wire on both coils in the same direction, and when the winding is completed give each a coat of shellac and lay aside until dry.

You will need to make a yoke for the magnets from a piece of heavy sheet iron. You can use the metal from a tin can if you use two thicknesses. The yoke should be about five-eighths of an inch wide and two and one-quarter inches long. Two one-quarter-inch holes through which to slip the ends of the magnet cores are bored in the yoke one inch apart. After the cores have been slipped through the holes in the yoke, a nut is screwed on the end of each so that the yoke is clamped between two nuts on each core.

When a horseshoe electromagnet such as that just described is connected to two or three dry cells it will lift a surprisingly heavy weight. A hammer or a large wrench are easily picked up.

Large electromagnets are made for lifting large castings and heavy pieces of iron in foundries. In mills where nails, bolts, etc., are made they can be picked up and handled by large lifting magnets at a great saving of labor over other methods.

Now that you have seen how an electric current can produce magnetism, here is an important thing to remember, and if you do, you will always be able to understand electricity much better.

Whenever we send electricity on an errand—to carry our voice over the telephone or a message over the telegraph—we can do so only because of the fact that electricity can produce magnetism. And when we ask electricity to do our work for us, to lift or move something or turn a heavy piece of machinery, electricity produces magnetism in responding to the task.

SENDING THE FIRST PUBLIC TELEGRAPH MESSAGE

CHAPTER FIVE

THE ELECTRIC TELEGRAPH, THE FIRST COMMERCIAL USE FOR ELECTRIC CURRENT

THE electromagnet and Volta's battery changed electricity from a curiosity and plaything into something useful. They first brought us the electric telegraph. Electricity did no useful work and earned no money until the electric telegraph was invented in 1837. Prior to the invention of the telegraph there was no dependable means of *rapid* communication over distances of more than a few miles. Messages could be sent only by courier or by signaling with bonfires, semaphores and other visible means. A courier could travel only as fast as his legs, a horse, a train or a boat would carry him. It required a long time for news to travel from one place to another in those days. All electrical industries have been established less than a century, probably after your great-grandfather was born. The telegraph opened new paths for the infant science of electricity—paths which led to the later development of the telephone, electric power, radio, television and the marvelous electronic era of today.

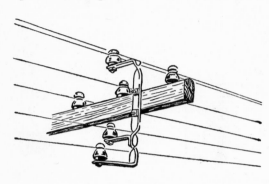

WIRES AROUND THE EARTH

Western Union Telegraph offices in the U. S. A. and the offices of corporations which lease wires from Western Union are connected by overhead wires, underground cables and microwave radio beams. If spliced together in one piece, the wires and cables would form a conductor long enough to go around the earth at the equator more than 50 times.

Many men, among them such prominent scientists as Oersted, Ampère, Gauss, Henry and Wheatstone, had ideas for sending messages by means of electricity and built short experimental telegraph lines. But there was something impractical about all their attempts until an artist—a portrait painter—found out how the thing could be done in the most practical way. The name of this artist-inventor, and even if he had never become famous as an inventor, he probably would have been remembered for his fine paintings, was Samuel Finley Breese Morse. He was born in Charlestown, Massachusetts, in April, 1791, and was graduated from Yale in 1810.

Morse was forty-one years old and teaching art at New York University when he built his first telegraph instruments. It was in October, 1832, while returning from a study of art in Europe, that Morse conceived the principle of his telegraph. A fellow passenger aboard the same ship showed Morse an electromagnet and demonstrated a number of experiments with it. During a discussion of the demonstrations Morse learned that the speed of electricity was believed to be instantaneous. From this fact Morse concluded that if he could arrange an electromagnet to detect a current of electricity, he could transmit signals rapidly between distant points. While still on shipboard, before arriving in New York, Morse designed his first telegraph "on paper."

Back at the university, the first working model was soon made from an old wooden frame such as artists use for stretching canvas, the wheels of a clock and a pair of electromagnets.

Pins

INSULATOR AND PINS

Telegraph and telephone wires are insulated from the poles by glass insulators which screw on wooden pins.

For several years the inventor expended much effort trying to convince the world that his telegraph would work and that it would have practical and commercial value. Since Morse depended upon his painting for a living he had practically no time or funds to build models of his invention for public exhibition. At last, in the fall of 1837, a working model was completed and placed in a large room at New York University, where numbers of people witnessed its operation. With the exception of Alfred Vail, a young student at the university through whom some money had been raised in return for a one-fourth interest in the invention, Morse could find no one who seemed to believe in him or his invention to the extent of risking dollars. It is the old story of genius contending with poverty. But after several years of struggle came success.

Morse, Alfred Vail and a third young entrepreneur (a travelling salesman for a patent plow, named Ezra Cornell, who later founded

Cornell University) built the first long-distance telegraph line in the world. It was built along the tracks of the Baltimore and Ohio Railroad between Baltimore, Maryland, and Washington, D. C., with money appropriated by the United States Congress.

It was over this line that Morse, on the morning of May 24, 1844, sent the historic first public telegram. It consisted of four words—"WHAT HATH GOD WROUGHT!"—a quotation from the Bible.

From this 40-mile experimental line between Baltimore and Washington the telegraph grew rapidly, especially in America. In 1846 the Baltimore-Washington line was extended to New York by Morse and his associates. Only seven years after Morse sent the first public message, over fifty telegraph companies were in operation in the United States. Some prospered, some failed and disap-

Sending news dispatches is an important part of telegraph service. A telegraph operator with key and sounder was once a familiar sight at big league baseball games and other important events. This operator, located in the grandstand, is clicking off a play-by-play description of a World Series ball game of forty years ago.

peared. It soon became obvious that a single large unified telegraph company could overcome many of the problems encountered by numerous smaller companies. Consolidation of the rival telegraph companies could not be accomplished until an enabling act was passed by the New York Legislature, April 4, 1856. The corporate title of the combined companies became "Western Union." With protection from harmful competition, the elimination of duplicate lines and offices and the use of the more efficient Morse devices, Western Union made rapid strides. The United States had been provided with its first national telegraph service. One of the epic achievements of American enterprise was the completion of the first transcontinental telegraph line in 1861. Until then the only fast communication between the East Coast and West Coast was by Pony Express. It required ten days for these couriers to carry mail and telegrams from the telegaph's western terminal at St. Joseph, Missouri, to Sacramento, California. The completion of the first transcontinental telegraph line threw the valiant group of riders into the discard.

To send a telegram half a century ago, it was customary to hand or telephone the message to a telegraph office. There a telegraph operator transmitted the message with a key or a "transmitting typewriter." The transmission was accomplished by making a series of dots and dashes corresponding to the Morse alphabet. The trained ear of an operator at the receiving apparatus translated the clicks of the receiving sounder into the letters and numerals of the alphabet.

For many decades almost all train dispatching and communication between railroad stations regarding traffic was handled by the key and sounder method. Today there is almost no place where one can find the old-fashioned Morse key and sounder clicking out the "dots" and "dashes" of the Morse code or alphabet.

At the turn of the century before there were moving-picture

theatres in every town, Boy Scout troops, radio sets, telephones, automobiles and the many other things boys of today are interested in, it was not easy to find a use for spare time and one of the hobbies of boys was telegraphing. They ran wires to the house next door, across the street, down the road or to the next farm—wherever they had friends. They made or bought telegraph instruments, learned the Morse code and soon were able to send messages back and forth.

The operation of a Morse telegraph line is not a complicated or a difficult matter to understand. The Morse telegraph system consisted of four things:

1. A battery to produce an electric current.
2. A wire to conduct the current from one telegraph station to another. One wire only was used when the earth was part of the circuit. (Two wires are necessary if the earth is not used.)
3. A key which works like a switch to turn the current on and off.
4. An electromagnet (or pair of electromagnets) which will move a lever and make a clicking noise when the electric current is shut on and off. This instrument is called the sounder.

THE MORSE KEY

is a simple contrivance for shutting the current off and on in much the same manner as an ordinary switch. It consists of a steel lever mounted on what are called "trunnion" screws. The two projections on the side of the old-fashioned muzzle-loading cannon were called "trunnions." The lever of a telegraph key swings up and down just like the barrels of the old cannon—that is, on trunnions. One end of the lever is provided with a rubber knob which the telegraph operator grasps with his thumb and forefinger. The other end of the lever is fitted with a screw to adjust the distance the lever can move up and down. On pressing the lever downward, a contact point (made of silver) fastened on the underside is brought into contact with another

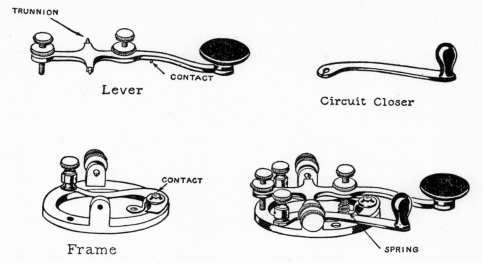

TRUNNION

CONTACT

Lever

Circuit Closer

CONTACT

Frame

SPRING

THE STANDARD MORSE TELEGRAPH KEY

silver contact point set in a rubber bushing on the base of the key, thus making an electrical connection or "closing the circuit" as it is sometimes called. When the telegraph operator takes the pressure of his fingers off the knob, a spring on the underside of the lever raises it, separating the contacts and "opening" or "breaking" the circuit as a telegraph operator would say. The key is also fitted with a lever called a circuit-closing lever which is nothing more or less than a switch which is kept closed whenever the key is not in use.

THE MORSE TELEGRAPH SOUNDER

A Morse telegraph sounder is really a small electric hammer. It consists of two electromagnets fastened to a base under a movable piece of iron called the armature. The armature is attracted by the electromagnets when a current flows through them and is pulled back by a spring when the current ceases. The iron armature is fastened to a brass rod called the lever. The lever strikes against a brass anvil and produces the clicks which form the dots and dashes of the Morse telegraph code.

The key and the sounder and a battery are connected in series and to the telegraph line. Every time the key is pressed, current from the battery flows over the line and through the electromagnets on the sounder. The electromagnets pull the armature down and the lever

A MORSE TELEGRAPH SOUNDER AND ITS PARTS

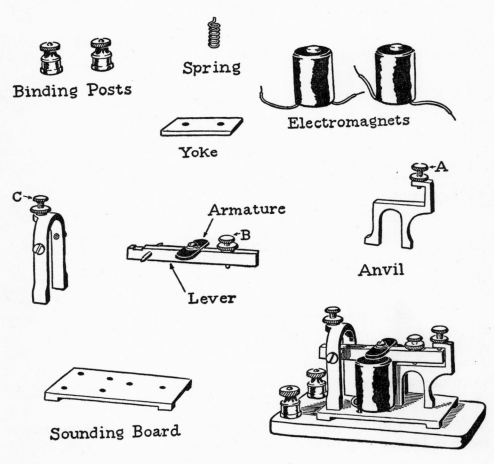

strikes the anvil and makes a click. When the key lever is released, the current flow ceases, the spring on the sounder pulls the lever up and it clicks against the top of the anvil.

The period of time between the first click and the second is controlled by the length of time the key lever is pressed down. A short period with the two clicks coming very close together is called a dot. A longer interval, equal to the time it would take to make three dots, is a dash. Combinations of dots and dashes arranged to represent each letter of the alphabet, numerals and punctuation marks, as in the "code" which Morse devised, make intelligent signals which it does not take long to memorize. A good telegraph operator receives and sends about thirty-five words a minute.

MORE THAN ONE MESSAGE MAY BE SENT OVER THE SAME WIRE AT THE SAME TIME

The cost of installing telegraph lines from one city to another amounts to a large sum of money. It requires a great many wires to carry all the telegraph messages between two cities. Consequently, wherever telegraph traffic is heavy and constant, "multiplex" systems for sending more than one message over the same wire at the same time are used. As many as eight can be sent simultaneously. By means of the "duplex" system two messages can be sent and with the "quadruplex" four. You may ask how this is done. Don't messages get mixed up? No, they don't. But you will need to know more about electricity than you can learn from this book before "multiplex" telegraphy can be explained to you.

THE MECHANIZATION OF TELEGRAPHY

Telegraph machines began to replace the Morse Code operator, key and sounder in 1915. It is not necessary to be trained in the

Morse code to operate these machines. No one receives the messages by ear and translates the clicks of a telegraph sounder into letters and numerals. Messages come out of the machines printed on a paper tape or on a sheet of paper in plain Roman characters. When a telegraph message is telephoned or delivered to a Western Union office it is typed by the operator on a keyboard similar to a typewriter keyboard.

SENDING A TELEGRAM BY
HIGH-SPEED AUTOMATIC MACHINE

Striking the keys punches holes in a narrow moving paper tape. Letters of the alphabet, numerals and other characters on the keyboard are represented by coded combinations of holes punched in the tape. The operator simply types a routing symbol at the beginning of each telegram and then types the message.

The coded routing symbol causes an "electronic brain" at a distant high-speed message center to route and flash the message to its destination area. The tape passes on through the transmitting machine where small pins slip in and out of the holes in the tape as they move past. The movement of the pins sends out electrical impulses over the telegraph line to the receiver. Upon reaching their destination, the electrical impulses are translated by the receiving machine into characters printed on a tape which the operator pastes on one of the familiar yellow telegraph blanks.

As a result of this highly-mechanized operation, telegrams and cablegrams now travel faster than ever before in telegraph history.

THE TELEPRINTER

Another device which has mechanized telegraphic communication is called the teleprinter. Telegrams are transmitted to and from Western Union offices around the country and from more than 23,000 business offices by means of the teleprinter. It is used on short lines and where traffic is light. Outgoing telegrams are typed by the operator on a typewriter-like keyboard. Incoming messages are received automatically in page form on the same machine.

TYPE 32 TELEX KEYBOARD MACHINE

This compact, streamlined telegram transmitter and receptor is installed in business offices in the major cities in the United States.

THE TELEPRINTER

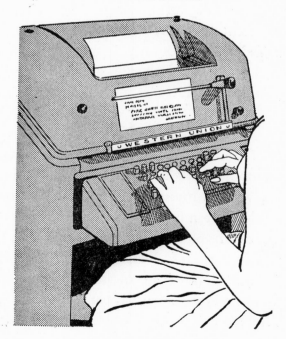

THE TYPE 32 TELEX KEYBOARD MACHINE

It is about the same size as an ordinary electric typewriter and so can be placed adjacent to a secretary's or receptionist's desk. The operation of the Telex requires only simple typing skill. Outgoing telegrams are typed by the operator on a typewriter-like keyboard. Incoming telegrams are received automatically in page form.

THE DESK-FAX

This ingenious facsimile machine sends and receives messages in "picture" form, automatically at the mere push of a button. When a drawing, picture, written message or "what-have-you" is dropped in the machine and a button is pushed, an electric eye scans the message or picture as it turns on a revolving cylinder and transmits over wire or radio beam a series of electrical impulses, corresponding to the light and dark portions of the message. A true reproduction is thereupon recorded on electro-sensitive paper at the distant receiving machine. The Desk-Fax is not much larger than a telephone desk set. The same machine both sends and receives pictures and telegrams.

HOW MESSAGES ARE CABLED ACROSS THE OCEAN

Until the year 1866, the only way of sending a message between Europe and America was by a letter or messenger travelling on a boat. No one could tell ahead of time how long it would take. Two weeks from New York to Liverpool on the fastest clipper ship would almost be a record—something which could be hoped for only once in a while. And then a ship could not always be found waiting and ready to sail. There might be a long delay before a message started. A great deal could happen on one side of the world and the other side would not know about it until at least two weeks later.

This was all changed when the first telegraph cable was laid across

THE DESK-FAX, A MACHINE WHICH SENDS TELEGRAMS BY PUSH BUTTON

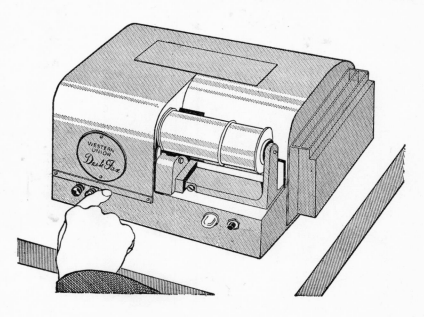

the Atlantic Ocean. Work was started in 1857. It was a tremendous undertaking. It was necessary first to manufacture a special cable in which the conducting wires were carefully protected by an outer sheath of insulating materials and a covering of metal armor. This cable, many hundreds of miles long, was then sunk to the bottom of the ocean between Valentia, Ireland, and Trinity Bay, Newfoundland. It was completed August 5, 1858. It lasted less than a month —until September 3. Then it broke down. It was not strong enough. Work was started on a new cable. In 1866, it was completed. This was the first successful Atlantic cable. Others soon followed and now a network of cables crisscrosses the bottoms of the oceans all over the world.

A telegraph sounder cannot be used to receive the messages sent

SIPHON–RECORDER

This machine prints the messages sent over ocean cables upon a paper tape. The message appears as a wavy line.

over an ocean cable. The current which travels through the cable when the key is pressed does not go to the other end instantly as it does over a telegraph line. It travels along like a wave. It takes one-fifth of a second for a signal to travel between Ireland and Newfoundland and then three seconds more for the current to gain its full strength. This makes a special device for receiving messages necessary.

HOW TO MAKE A TELEGRAPH KEY AND SOUNDER

When Thomas A. Edison was a very young man—before he became known as an inventor, he was a telegraph operator. When he was about eleven years old he started experimenting with chemistry. In order to earn money to buy the things he needed for his experiments, he went to work when he was twelve years old selling newspapers, candy, fruit, etc., on the Grand Trunk Railroad between Port Huron and Detroit. It was while he was a newsboy on the railroad that Edison became interested in electricity, probably from visiting telegraph offices with a chum of similar tastes.

This interest in electricity led the two boys to build a telegraph line between their homes. Their homemade telegraph instruments were rather crude. Iron wire fastened to bottles set on nails driven into trees and low poles furnished the line. It was thus that Thomas A. Edison, who was destined to make many important telegraph inventions, first mastered the rudiments of the art of telegraphy.

It is not difficult to build a simple telegraph key and sounder. You can use the electromagnets described in the last chapter. You will need to mount them on a wooden base. The ends of the cores pass through two holes in the base and are clamped in place by two nuts.

The armature is made out of heavy galvanized iron. A piece of

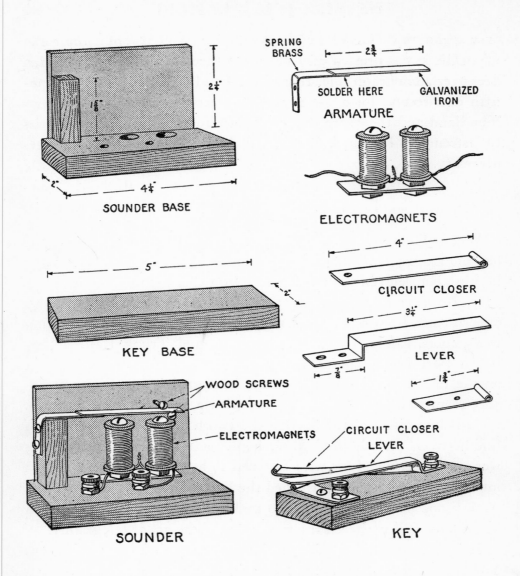

SPRING BRASS

SOLDER HERE

GALVANIZED IRON

2¾"

ARMATURE

2¼"

SOUNDER BASE

2"

4¼"

1⅝"

ELECTROMAGNETS

5"

2"

KEY BASE

CIRCUIT CLOSER

4"

3¼"

LEVER

⅞"

1¼"

WOOD SCREWS

ARMATURE

ELECTROMAGNETS

CIRCUIT CLOSER

LEVER

SOUNDER

KEY

EXPERIMENTS WITH ELECTROMAGNETISM

These sketches show how to make a telegraph key and sounder.

thin spring brass is soldered or riveted to one end of the armature. The other end of the spring is screwed to the top of a little wooden block of just the right height so that the armature comes directly over the magnets and about one-eighth of an inch above them. The opposite end of the armature moves up and down for about an eighth of an inch between two "anvil" screws. One of these screws is on the wooden back (a piece of cigar-box wood) and the other is a short distance below it. The screws should be adjusted so that the armature can move up and down between them for about an eighth of an inch.

The spring attached to the armature should be adjusted by bending so as to raise the armature up and away from the magnets when the current is not flowing. If the spring is not strong enough attach a small rubber band or a light wire spring to the armature so as to help lift it.

Galvanized iron, sheet tin or brass strips one-half an inch wide can be used for making the key. Cut and bend these according to the plan in the illustration. The key parts should be mounted on a wooden base about three by four inches. The metal strip which forms the key lever is arranged so that when it is pressed, it will touch and make contact with the head of a brass screw on the contact strip. The lever should be bent so that it has enough spring to rise up off the screw on the contact strip as soon as released from the pressure of the fingers. A round-headed screw passing through a clearance hole in the lever will prevent it from rising too far.

One edge of the contact strip is bent up just far enough so that the circuit-closing lever will slide underneath.

In order to set the key and sounder up for code practice, you will need a dry cell or homemade Leclanché cell like that described in Chapter Four. Connect the apparatus as in the diagram. Always keep the circuit-closer lever "open," that is, away from the contact

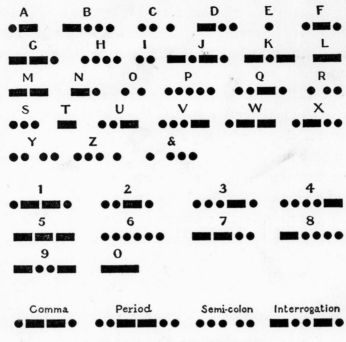

MORSE TELEGRAPH ALPHABET

strip, or the battery current will be wasted. The circuit closer is used only when two keys and sounders are connected to the same line.

Pressing the key should cause the battery current to flow through the sounder magnets and draw the armature down so that it makes a "click." Releasing the key lever will open the circuit so that the armature flies back up and makes another click.

The first thing to do when learning to telegraph is to memorize the Morse code so that you know the symbols for each letter of the alphabet. It will help you to remember them if you look the code over and find out which symbols are the reverse of the others. For example "A" is the reverse of "N."

SWITCH

SOUNDER

A   B

DRY
CELL

B   A

KEY

CLOSE TO RECEIVE
OPEN TO SEND

EXPERIMENTS WITH ELECTROMAGNETISM

The upper sketch shows a complete telegraph system set up between neighboring houses. In the center is the circuit arrangement. The lower sketch shows how to connect a single key and sounder for code practice.

A "dot" is made by pressing the key down and releasing it the instant that it touches the contact screw. A "dash" is made by pressing the key down and holding it down for about the same length of time as it would take to make three dots. Some of the letters, "O, C, R, Y, and Z," have a space in them. The space interval is supposed to be just a bit longer than a dot.

If you make two keys and sounders you can set them up on opposite sides of a room or in two different rooms and so have two stations. You will need two double contact switches. You can make the switches yourself. One of the illustrations also shows how to connect the instruments. The circuit-closing levers should be kept closed and the switch levers kept on the contacts marked B whenever you are not sending or receiving messages. Otherwise current will be wasted and the battery will become exhausted. The positive and negative terminals of the battery are shown in the illustration. You should take notice of these and connect the instruments exactly as shown. You will probably need two cells of battery at each end of the line and should not use a wire smaller than No. 18 as the "line."

CHAPTER SIX

ELECTRIC BELLS, WIRES, AND SOMETHING ABOUT
ELECTRICAL MEASUREMENTS

ONE of the smaller things that electromagnetism does for us every day is ring our doorbell. The common form of electric bell (they were once called electric *trembling* bells), consists of an electromagnet which moves a hammer or tapper back and forth so that it beats against a gong. It is a simple little device but just like almost everything else someone had to think of it. A man named John Mirand invented the electric bell in 1850.

ELECTRIC BELL

The diagram at the left shows how this simple but useful electrical device operates. The diagram at the right shows how a doorbell, battery, and push button are connected.

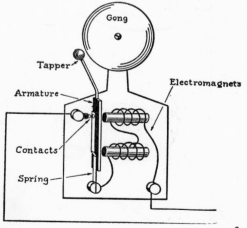

HOW ELECTROMAGNETISM RINGS A DOORBELL

An electric buzzer is made exactly like an electric bell except that it has no gong and hammer. This is how the bell works:

An iron armature carrying a little hammer is arranged in front of two electromagnets so that when a current of electricity flows through the electromagnets, the armature is drawn towards them and the hammer strikes the gong. When the armature moves towards the electromagnets a short distance it separates two contact points which are part of the circuit. This "breaks" or interrupts the circuit so that the current ceases to flow and the magnetism disappears. A spring pushes the armature back away from the magnets and brings the contacts together again. When the contacts touch, the current can flow again and strike the hammer against the

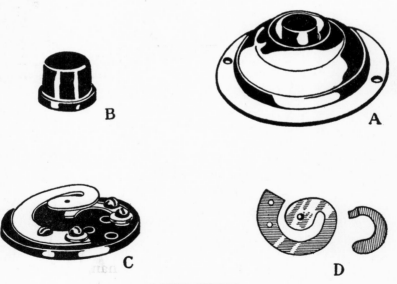

A PUSH BUTTON

A push button is actually a small switch. *A* is the complete push. *B* is the "button" which pushes the contacts together. The contacts are marked *D*. The assembled parts without the cover are shown at *C*.

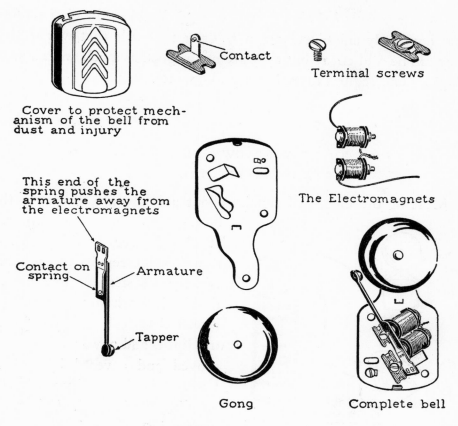

Cover to protect mech-
anism of the bell from
dust and injury

Contact

Terminal screws

This end of the
spring pushes the
armature away from
the electromagnets

The Electromagnets

Contact on
spring — Armature

Tapper

Gong

Complete bell

AN ELECTRIC DOORBELL

bell. This process keeps on repeating itself as long as the "button"
is pushed. In an electric buzzer, it is the armature, vibrating back
and forth, which makes the buzzing sound.

PUSH BUTTONS

Push buttons are nothing more or less than a very simple form
of switch. Pressing the button moves a spring against a contact
point and closes the circuit.

There are some bells made nowadays and sold in the chain stores, that have only one electromagnet. They are made that way so that they can be sold cheap but they are not as good as a bell with double magnets and require more battery to operate.

HOW TO BE YOUR OWN ELECTRICIAN AND
REPAIR AN ELECTRIC BELL

Most of the electrical repairs about a house are distinctly the business of a licensed electrician. It would be very foolish for a boy to undertake repairs to the electric light system or to some of the devices which connect with it. All electrical wiring for electric lights and power must be approved and covered by a Fire Underwriter's Certificate if the building is insured. Otherwise it may invalidate the insurance.

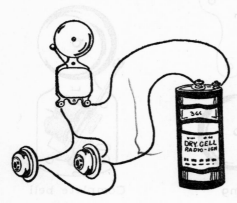

BELL CIRCUIT

Sometimes it is desirable to ring a bell from two different push buttons. This shows how the circuit is arranged.

However, it should not be necessary to call in an electrician to repair or install an electric bell when there is a handy boy around who knows something about electricity.

The three most common reasons why a bell or buzzer sometimes fails to operate are:

1. A weak or exhausted battery, or a power failure if a bell transformer is used
2. A broken circuit
3. Mechanical derangement of the bell or push button

Unless the wires in the bell circuit are very short, more than one cell of battery should be used. The dry cell known as a **No. 6** is best. Use two cells for an ordinary doorbell system and three cells when the lines are long.

When a bell fails to operate and you are certain that it is not the fault of the battery look for the trouble in the circuit, in the bell and push button. The following list of possible causes of trouble may be of assistance.

1. Exhausted battery, or no power at transformer
2. Weak or insufficient battery
3. Cells not properly connected, positive to negative, etc
4. Bad connection to battery terminals, bell or push button
5. Broken wire
6. Dirty contact points on the bell
7. Dirty contacts or broken spring on push button
8. Spring on bell out of adjustment
9. Armature or tapper stuck
10. Short circuit in the wiring

It is sometimes desirable to arrange a bell with two or more push buttons at different points so that any one of them will ring the bell or a bell and a buzzer that may be operated by the same battery. The diagrams will show you how to do these things.

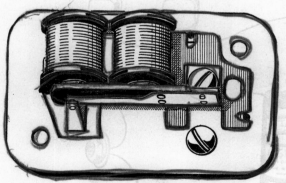

A BUZZER

A buzzer may be said to be a bell without a gong and tapper.

SOMETHING ABOUT
WIRES

All sorts of wires and cables are necessary in

order to lead electricity from place to place. When they stretch from pole to pole and must carry their own weight, they are usually made of "hard-drawn" copper wire which is stronger than "soft-drawn" wire. Soft-drawn wire conducts electricity better and is used when there is no weight to be supported.

Wires supported from poles are often bare and are insulated from the pole by glass or porcelain knobs called insulators.

The telephone wires leading into a house or building are insulated with rubber and cotton which has been saturated with chemicals to improve the insulation and protect from the effects of weather. These wires are always twisted.

The electric light wires leading into a building or a house are also insulated with rubber and cotton like a telephone wire but may run parallel to each other. Sometimes two wires insulated with rubber and fabric are bound together under a layer of cotton. This is

A BELL AND A BUZZER MAY BE OPERATED FROM
THE SAME BATTERY OR TRANSFORMER

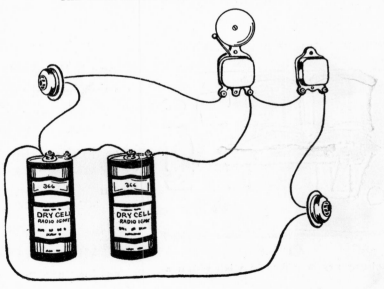

INSULATORS

Here are some of the many forms of insulators used to support wires so the current will not leak.

"duplex" wire. Insulated wires made for use outdoors are called "weatherproof."

The electric light and power wires running underground are covered or insulated with rubber and fabric and are in fact weatherproof wires but are further protected by running them through insulating tubes called fibre conduits, made of wood pulp or chopped up newspapers saturated with asphaltum or some other waterproof insulating compound.

The telephone companies use both overhead and underground cables made up of a bundle of copper wires insulated with paraffined paper and enclosed in a lead tube.

The wires used to carry a current from an outlet to a lamp, or some electrical appliance, which must be flexible are called cords. They are "stranded," that is, made up of a number of small wires so as to bend more easily than a single solid wire, and are covered with a layer of rubber and cotton or silk.

The wires used in winding the coils and electromagnets which form an important part of many electrical machines are called magnet wires. They are made of soft-drawn copper and are insulated with a thin covering of silk, cotton or enamel. Sometimes a combination of these insulating coverings is used.

Wires are made in various sizes according to a scale known as Brown and Sharpe's gauge, usually abbreviated to B. & S. gauge.

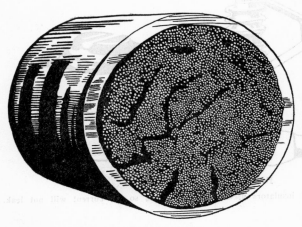

TELEPHONE CABLE

This lead tube 2⅝ inches in diameter contains 3,636 insulated wires. Cables have removed pole lines from main thoroughfares of large cities and reduced the size of poles where poles are still used.

ELECTRICAL MEASUREMENTS

The next few pages of this book may not be as interesting as some of the others for there are no experiments described. It is, however, one of the most important parts of the book for the boy who really wants to understand something about the fundamentals of electricity.

You will no doubt remember from stories which you have read that the American Indians used to measure time by "suns and moons." A "sun" was of course our *day* and a "moon" was four weeks or what we call a *lunar month*. The Indians spoke of long distances in terms of a day's journey. A day's journey, a sun and a moon were methods of measurement. One of the standards by which we compare one stage of civilization with another is the methods of measurement used.

It would be very difficult to make anything, to buy or sell or even talk about things for long without some system of measure-
ment which everyone understood. Everything must be
measured at some time or other.
It may be seconds, days, ounces,
grams, inches, centimeters,
pounds, or miles, or by some
special system, but nevertheless
it must be measured. Measuring is simply a means of comparing things with some
known standards. Some things
must be identified by two measurements. There are things
which we cannot see but which
can be measured. Time cannot
be seen but can be measured in
seconds, minutes, hours, days,
weeks, months and years. Heat
is invisible but can be measured in calories. Energy can
be measured in ergs and horsepower. Measurements give us
a more definite idea of things

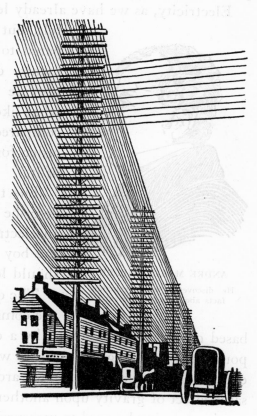

TELEPHONE WIRES

Before underground cables solved the problem, hundreds of telephone wires ran through the main streets on poles. These lines were easily damaged by winter storms and the telephone service was often interrupted by broken wires.

that we want to deal with. Some things must be identified by more than one measurement or standard of comparison. For instance, a man may be said to be six feet tall and to weigh 150 pounds. That description gives us a definite idea of a tall slender man—a far different person from one described as six feet tall and weighing 300 pounds.

Electricity, as we have already learned, cannot be seen, heard or felt, but it can be measured and compared to a standard. So can the instruments, circuits and conductors which provide a path for electricity. Somewhat like a man, electricity must also be compared to more than one standard in order for us to get a very definite idea of it.

ANDRE MARIE AMPERE
He discovered many valuable facts about electric currents.

The terms and measurements used to describe the qualities and properties of an electric current are something which the boy who is interested in electricity should learn to understand.

The quart and liter are units of measure commonly applied to liquids and are based on the space occupied by a certain volume of a liquid. The pound and the kilogram measure weight or the force which gravity exerts in pulling a substance toward the earth as compared with the same effect of gravity upon another standard "weight." Inches and centimeters can be used to measure size.

HOW ELECTRICAL VOLUME IS MEASURED

Electricity, being invisible and weightless, cannot be measured by any of the standards used for anything else. An inch, an ounce, or a liter will not serve. The only way of measuring electricity is by means of some of the effects which it produces. Its chemical, heating or electromagnetic abilities must be used as the basis of a system of measurement.

The first method used to measure an electrical current was the chemical one.

WHAT IS THE AMPERE?

When an electric current is passed through the proper chemical solution containing silver by means of two silver plates, silver will be deposited on one plate and dissolved from the other. If the electric current is supplied by a battery, the silver will be deposited on the plate connected to the zinc or *negative* pole of the battery. It will be dissolved from the plate connected to the carbon or *positive* pole. If the current is allowed to flow for a short time and the two silver plates are then taken out of the solution and weighed, it will be found that one plate is considerably heavier than the

THE FIRST ELECTRIC LIGHT METER

Edison made use of the chemical action of an electric current in his first meters. The zinc plates in the jars were taken out and weighed each month. The change in weight indicated how much current had been consumed and how much the customer owed.

other. The silver has been removed from one plate and deposited upon the other by the action of the electric *current*. An electric current which will deposit .06708 grams of silver in an hour is called an ampere. The ampere is the unit of measurement for an electrical current and is used to indicate the quantity or volume of the current.

The water running out of the low tank

does not have as much **voltage**

or **pressure** as the stream

from the tall one

VOLTAGE

Voltage and pressure are not exactly the same thing but if you have in mind the pressure of a stream of water when thinking of an electric current you will have an idea of what the voltage of an electric current is.

Edison used this simple principle in the meters which were installed for each customer of his first electric light plant. In a glass jar two zinc plates were immersed in a solution of zinc sulfate. A certain definite portion of the current used on the premises for lighting was passed through this meter and once a month the device was removed and another left in its stead. The plates which were removed were taken to a meter room where they were washed, dried and weighed on a chemical balance. Then on the basis of the amount of zinc removed from one plate and deposited on another, the bill was rendered for electric current. Owing to the fact that the zinc sulfate solution would freeze, the meter included an electric lamp to keep the solution warm. The lamp was automatically turned on by a thermostat whenever the temperature dropped to 40 degrees Fahrenheit or below. It is said that during cold weather, people would call up the Edison Company and, not knowing what the lamp was for, report that their meter was red hot. In time the *elec-*

The stream from the tall tank has more
voltage or **pressure** but the
stream from the low tank
has more **amperage** or **volume**

trolytic meter, as it was called, was replaced by the mechanical type which is in use today.

One of the best ways to understand certain things about an electric current is to imagine it a stream of water flowing through a pipe.

In order for a stream of water to flow through a pipe it must have pressure behind it. Otherwise it would not move. If you hold your thumb over the nozzle of a water faucet and turn on the water, you can easily feel the pressure which the water exerts.

An electrical current also exerts a pressure. It must have this pressure in order to move. The pressure of a stream of water enables it to overcome the resistance it meets in the walls of a pipe, and pass through small openings. The resistance of an electrical circuit is of course of a different nature from the frictional resistance of a pipe but it is overcome by electrical pressure.

Water pressure is measured in pounds but electrical pressure is measured in volts. When it is necessary to speak of very small fractions of a volt the words millivolt and microvolt are used.

1,000 millivolts equal one volt.

1,000,000 microvolts equal one volt.

Electricity has preserved the names of some of its most famous workers in the words used to express its volume, pressure, etc.

The ampere, the unit of electric current, is named after Andre M. Ampère, the French physicist (born 1775), who discovered many valuable things about the motion of electric currents. The volt, the unit of electrical pressure, is named after Alessandro Volta, the Italian physicist. The ohm, unit of electrical resistance, took its name from Georg S. Ohm, the German physicist who discovered the laws of resistance.

A volt may be measured by the effects it produces. It is most easily measured by the amount of electric current it will force through a certain amount of resistance. A volt is the unit of electrical force or pressure which will cause a current of one ampere to flow

746

Watts

Equal

<u>One</u>   Horsepower

WATTS

Electrical engineers do not pay much attention to "horsepower." They think in terms of watts, kilowatts, and kilovolt-amperes which are terms having a more definite meaning. A one-horsepower electric motor uses 746 watts.

150 Watts

will do

the Work

of

One Man

MAN POWER

Although a man can exert more than one-sixth of a horsepower for a short time, one-sixth of
a horsepower is about the limit of his energy when it is continuously applied.

through a resistance of one ohm. Five volts will force five amperes
through one ohm.

You may have heard the word voltage used at times. It is equivalent to saying "electrical pressure." Two other words which sometimes appear in scientific books and mean the same thing are potential and electromotive force.

There are of course other units of measurement used in electrical
science besides the volt, ampere and ohm, but only one other with
which the young experimenter need concern himself. It is the *watt*.
You will often see this word stamped on the name plate of some
electrical device. For example, lamps are marked 40 watts, 100
watts; flatirons, 600 watts, etc. A watt is the unit of electrical
power and if you know how many watts a lamp consumes or a flatiron uses you know how much electrical energy is required to operate it.

A watt is represented by a current of one ampere flowing through
a wire at a potential of one volt.

The number of watts is found by multiplying the number of amperes by the number of volts. If a lamp uses one ampere of current at 120 volts it consumes 120 watts. A flatiron which is marked 120 volts, 700 watts, will give you the clue to how many amperes pass through the iron at 120 volts. Divide 700 watts by 120 volts and the answer is 5.83 amperes. If you want to know how many ohms resistance the iron has, divide the volts by the amperes. The answer in this case would be 20.6.

WATT–HOUR METER

The electric-light meter is a watt-hour meter. It is an electric motor connected to the wiring in a house or building so that it changes its speed in proportion to the current consumed.

Seven hundred and forty-six watts represent one electrical horsepower. A quarter-horsepower motor uses about 190 watts. One thousand watts are called a kilowatt.

It is often necessary to know how much current is flowing in a circuit and at what voltage. This is done with instruments called "meters," whose name comes from a Latin word, *metrum*, which means a measure. There are all sorts and sizes of meters ranging from the cheap little affair on the dashboard of an automobile to the delicate and expensive instruments used in precision laboratory work. Some of them are made more carefully than a watch.

An instrument designed to measure electromotive force (electrical pressure) is called a voltmeter. An instrument designed to measure the volume of current is called an ammeter. Some meters do both and show the amount of electrical energy passing through a circuit. They are called wattmeters.

1-w

4-w

½-w

800-w

550-w

15-250-w

500-w

500-w

1000-w

3223

PENNSYLVANIA

3223

2,500,000 WATTS

HOW MUCH ENERGY IS REQUIRED

The amount of electrical energy required to operate electrical machines varies greatly. A flashlight bulb may require as little as ½-watt. On the other hand, a Class GG-1 Pennsylvania electric locomotive uses about 2,450,000 watts when pulling sixteen 85-ton passenger cars at 80 miles per hour on straight level track. Toy models of this type of locomotive use about 40 watts.

CHAPTER SEVEN

HOW HEAT IS PRODUCED BY ELECTRICITY AND ELECTRICITY IS MADE TO OBEY

STOP a moment and think of all the things which are operated by electricity in your home, in your school, along the streets or in some of the factories that you have visited. You can probably make quite a long list, which will be something like this:

Bells, buzzers, telephones, telegraphs, electric lights, fire alarms, automobiles, toasters, washing machines, flatirons, trolley cars, fans, heaters, stoves, soldering irons, coffee grinders, meat choppers, elevators, drill presses, saws, printing presses, and so on. Electricity is used for so many different purposes today, if you can think of one-half of them you will have a list which would fill several pages of this book. Then if you happen to know how such things as the telegraph and telephone operate, you probably will be able to pick out many of the electrical devices which contain coils of wire or electromagnets and are operated by electromagnetism. You can make up a new list which would start this way:

Bells, buzzers, telephones, telegraphs, fire alarms, automobiles, washing machines, trolley cars, fans, coffee grinders, meat choppers, elevators, drill presses, saws, printing presses, and so on.

You will have to leave electric lights, toasters, flatirons, heaters, stoves, soldering irons, etc., out of the list and put them in one by themselves because none of these depend upon electromagnetism for their operation. When an electric current flows through a wire or a piece of metal, magnetism is not the only thing that it produces.

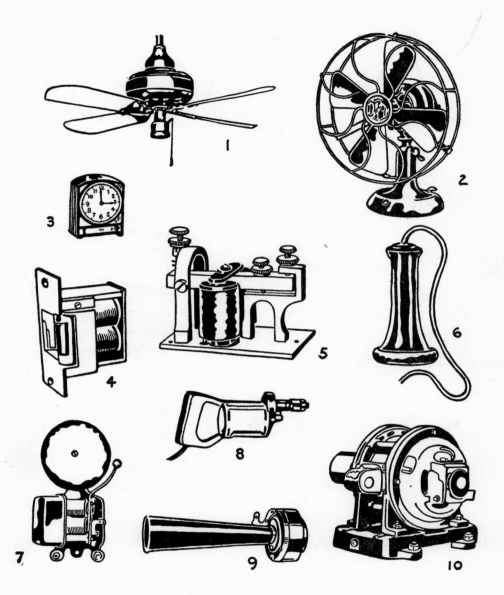

ELECTRICAL DEVICES USING ELECTROMAGNETS

Electrical machines which move in any manner depend upon electromagnetism to produce the motion. The devices shown in the illustration all employ electromagnets. 1 and 2 are fans. 3 is an electric clock, 4 a door-opener, 5 a telegraph sounder, 6 a telephone receiver, 7 an electric bell, 8 a drill, 9 an auto horn, 10 an electric motor.

ELECTRICAL DEVICES EMPLOYING THE HEATING
EFFECT OF AN ELECTRIC CURRENT

It produces *heat* as well, and it is this heat which is used to make electric lights, toasters, etc., operate.

When riding in an automobile you prefer a good smooth road made of concrete to travel upon. So does electricity prefer a certain kind of road or path over which to travel. Electricity prefers a metal. But not all metals offer the same smooth road to electricity.

An electric current finds it much easier travelling through a road made of silver than one of the same size made of tin or lead. The more scientific way of saying this would be: silver conducts electricity better than iron or lead. If we had the right sort of instruments for testing various metals it would be very easy to find out which ones offer electricity the best path or *are the best conductors*. But this has been carefully done thousands of times in well-equipped laboratories and the results published in many books. The best conductor is silver, the next best is copper. Next to copper comes gold, and so on down the list which follows, the substances at the bottom being the poorest conductors and offering the greatest *resistance* to the passage of an electric current. Electricity has to struggle to overcome the resistance of a poor conductor and *develops heat* during the effort. If someone tried to prevent you from passing along a road and you had to do a great deal of pushing and shoving to get by, the extra exertion would make you warm. You would develop heat. It is the same thing in the case of an electric current.

CONNECTORS

Connectors and terminals are used in electrical work to aid in making a good connection of low resistance.

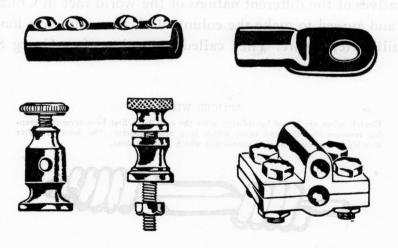

A list of metals arranged to show the best and poorest conductors.

Silver	Iron
Copper	Platinum
Gold	Nickel
Aluminum	Tin
Zinc	Lead

It always simplifies scientific matters a great deal if they can be dealt with in figures instead of words. Some of you won't agree but nevertheless it is a fact. If you are one of those boys who will some day go to college and study engineering, you will then learn a great deal about mathematics that you do not know now. When you become an engineer you will find figures to be your best friend. In order to deal with electricity in figures instead of in words, scientists and engineers had to find a way of measuring the *resistance* of an electrical circuit. They found a number of ways and then in order to have some sort of a unit for measuring resistance, the same as an ounce or pound is a unit for measuring weight, they decided to call the resistance of a certain sized column of mercury one *ohm*. Representatives of the different nations of the world met in Chicago in 1893 and agreed to make the column 106.30 centimeters long and one millimeter square. They called it an ohm after Georg Simon

SPLICED WIRES

Electric wires are joined by splicing after the ends have first been scraped. Scraping removes the dirt and oxide which is a non-conductor. The joint or splice is soldered to insure a good connection which will not heat.

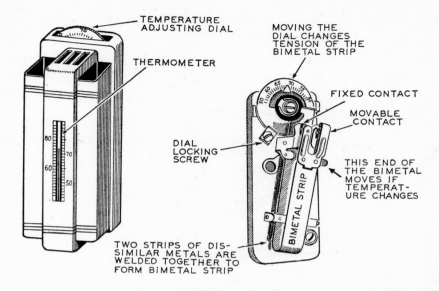

TEMPERATURE
ADJUSTING DIAL

MOVING THE
DIAL CHANGES
TENSION OF THE
BIMETAL STRIP

THERMOMETER

FIXED CONTACT

MOVABLE
CONTACT

DIAL
LOCKING
SCREW

THIS END OF
THE BIMETAL
MOVES IF
TEMPERAT-
URE CHANGES

BIMETAL STRIP

TWO STRIPS OF DIS-
SIMILAR METALS ARE
WELDED TOGETHER TO
FORM BIMETAL STRIP

A THERMOSTAT IS A SWITCH
WHICH IS OPERATED BY CHANGES IN TEMPERATURE

The room temperature in buildings cooled by air-conditioning machinery or heated by furnaces equipped with oil-burners or coal stokers is automatically regulated by a thermostat. A thermostat consists of a strip of bimetal which moves in one direction when it becomes warmer and in the opposite direction when it is cooled. The metal strip is fitted with contacts which are part of an electric circuit. Movements of the strip open and close the circuit. The thermostat is adjustable so that it will open or close a circuit and thus stop or start a cooling or heating plant at any desired temperature.

The temperature in an electric refrigerator is regulated by a thermostat. Electric blankets and heating pads are also equipped with thermostats so that the heating current is shut off automatically before the blanket or pad becomes too hot and is turned on again before too much cooling occurs.

Ohm, a famous scientist who contributed a great deal to our knowledge of electricity.

Electricity always develops a certain amount of heat in its travels. There is no such thing as a perfect conductor of electricity. Everything offers some resistance, even silver and copper. Electric motors are wound with copper wire but they become warm when electricity passes through them. A copper wire which is "overloaded," a term the electrical engineer uses to mean "carrying too much current," becomes very hot—sometimes hot enough to melt.

A wire made of iron or lead will become much hotter than a

copper wire of the same size. But lead and iron are not ideal substances to use in making resistance wires for heating electric flatirons, toasters, etc. Lead melts easily and iron oxidizes or rusts. So alloys are made for the purpose. Alloys are mixtures of two or more metals. The most widely used alloy is called Nichrome. It is a mixture made of the purest nickel and chromium available. It is made into wires and ribbons which have more than fifty times the resistance of a copper wire or ribbon of the same size.

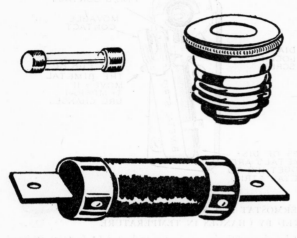

FUSES

There are many different sizes and types of fuses. Here are the most common ones. The fuse in the glass tube is used in radios, automobiles, and electrical instruments. The cartridge fuse is used in circuits carrying heavy currents. The plug fuse is the type used for house lighting.

If you look closely at an electric toaster you will find the heating element which becomes red hot when the current is turned on. It may be a wire wound in a long spiral or a flat ribbon woven around a strip of mica. It is probably made of Nichrome. Below is a list of some of the devices which depend upon a heating unit of some sort and probably using Nichrome.

Electric heaters

Electric stoves

Electric flatirons

Electric percolators

Electric waffle-irons

Electric toasters

Electric soldering irons

Electric sterilizers

Electric furnaces

Electric curling irons

Electric gluepots

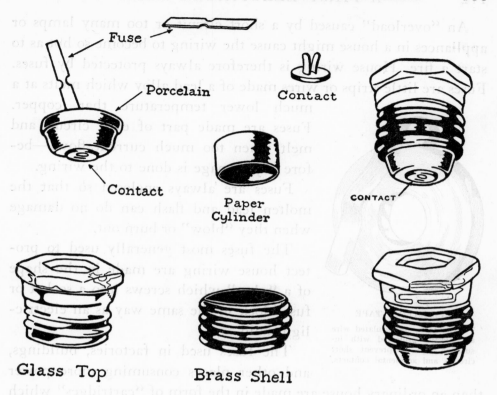

Fuse

Porcelain

Contact

Contact

Paper
Cylinder

CONTACT

Glass Top

Brass Shell

A FUSE PLUG SEPARATED INTO ITS PARTS

WHAT A FUSE IS FOR

Since electricity can heat a copper wire just as well as a resistance wire when too much current flows in a circuit, some means of preventing this is necessary, and so all power circuits are fitted with some sort of fuse or cutout. A cutout, also called a circuit breaker, is an automatic switch operated by electromagnets. It opens and shuts off the electricity where there is an "overload" or too much current flowing.

An "overload" caused by a short circuit or too many lamps or appliances in a house might cause the wiring to become so hot as to start a fire. House wiring is therefore always protected by fuses. Fuses are little strips or wires made of a lead alloy which melts at a much lower temperature than copper. Fuses are made part of each circuit and melt when too much current flows—before any damage is done to the wiring.

INSULATING TAPE

The joints in an insulated wire are always protected with insulating tape to prevent short circuits and accidental contacts.

Fuses are always enclosed so that the molten lead and flash can do no damage when they "blow" or burn out.

The fuses most generally used to protect house wiring are made in the shape of a "plug" which screws into a socket or fuse block in the same way as an electric-light bulb.

The fuses used in factories, buildings, and other places consuming more power than an ordinary house are made in the form of "cartridges" which snap into spring holders.

All fuses are made in different sizes.

An automobile without a steering wheel, a clutch or a throttle would not be of much use. It has to be controlled. It must stop and go ahead at the right time. Electricity too must be controlled. It must stop and start at the right time. Otherwise it would be of little use. Engineers have given a great deal of attention to building the proper devices for controlling an electric current. They have developed all sorts of switches, rheostats, circuit breakers and other instruments for controlling the strength of an electric current and for shutting it on and off completely.

SWITCHES

If we cut a wire through which a current is flowing, the electricity must stop. When the ends of the wire are joined again, the current can flow once more. That is what a switch does. An electric switch opens and closes an electric circuit. When a switch is "open," there is a gap in the circuit which the electric current cannot pass. Closing a switch removes the gap so that the current can flow again. The simple act of pressing your finger on a little knob can stop or start an electrical process miles away.

The little push button which, when pressed, causes a doorbell to ring, is an electric switch. Push buttons are made in all sorts of shapes and sizes but they are all simply small switches and operate in the same manner. Pressing a button forces a spring against a little contact and closes the circuit. When the pressure is removed, the spring opens the circuit.

The telegraph key is another form of switch made for the special purpose of opening and closing a circuit very rapidly under the delicate control of a telegraph operator's fingers.

The switches set in the wall and used to turn the electric lights on and off are designed and built for that particular duty. They are all of the type called snap switches. That is actually what they do—snap open and closed. There is a good reason for this. Every time a circuit or a switch is opened a spark takes place. If the switch is opened slowly the spark may develop into a flame which would injure the switch and might even cause a fire. When a switch is opened very rapidly there is no chance for the flame to develop and the spark is kept very small and harmless. Electric light switches are used very frequently and are made to snap open and closed in order to be more durable and for the sake of safety.

The switches used to open or close circuits through which heavy currents of electricity flow must be large or they would become hot. A switch made to carry a current of 2,000 amperes is quite a heavy affair.

SWITCHES

There are many different forms of switches and devices for controlling an electric current. 1, 5, 7, 8 and 9 are "snap" switches. 2 is a telegraph key, 3 is a telephone transmitter, 4 a push button, 6 a knife switch, 10 and 11 motor-starting devices and 12 a sign flasher.

AUTOMATIC CIRCUIT-BREAKER

Modern homes often are provided with a cir-cuit-breaker which eliminates all fuses. If the wiring becomes overloaded, the breaker mechanism automatically opens a switch.

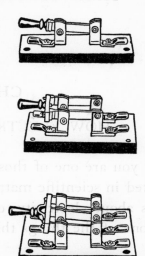

KNIFE SWITCHES

This type of switch is used on switchboards to control large amounts of electric current.

When high voltages and large currents must be turned on and off as in a power house, oil-immersed switches are used. The switch itself is actually kept submerged in a tank of oil but provided with an exposed handle so that it may be manipulated. Oil is a very good insulator and when the switch is opened, it quenches the spark and flame caused by opening the circuit.

When several large switches must be operated simultaneously as in a power house, they are motor driven. Opening or closing a small switch connected with the motor thus controls several large pieces of mechanism instantly.

ⓒ The sketch of the Automatic Circuit-breaker is from *Home Electrical Repairs*, copyright, 1950, by Alfred P. Morgan. By permission of Crown Publishers.

CHAPTER EIGHT

HOW ELECTRICITY TRANSMITS SPEECH

IF you are one of those boys who are destined to be always interested in scientific matters, you will probably read a great many books about electricity, chemistry and physics as you grow older and one of the things that you will learn is that almost all great inventions have been the result of long and careful study on the part of many workers rather than the sudden inspiration of a single genius.

ALEXANDER GRAHAM BELL
He invented the first practical
telephone instrument.

Alexander Graham Bell invented the telephone, but he was only able to do so because other men like Alessandro Volta, Hans Oersted, Michael Faraday, Humphry Davy, William Sturgeon, and Johann Reis first found out how to make batteries and electromagnets and discovered facts about electricity which Bell could use in making a telephone.

The first man to build an instrument which was anything like the present telephone was a professor of physics in the little town of Friedrichsdorf, far up in the northern part of Germany between Russia and the Baltic Sea. His name was Johann P. Reis and in 1861 he made several very ingenious instruments according to a plan which had been published in a French magazine seven years before by a young soldier named Charles Bourseul. Reis's telephones had a small fault in the transmitter, however, which prevented them from operating as well as they might have. This pioneer did not understand how complicated the sounds of the human voice are and the transmitter which he built would send only what is called the *pitch*[1] of a sound over the wires. It could not transmit words. A very small change, merely the proper adjustment of a screw, would have made this possible but Reis did not know it and so he missed the chance of becoming wealthy and **famous** by a very small margin.

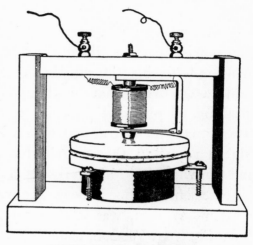

BELL'S FIRST TELEPHONE

Bell, the man who finally made the first telephone which would actually talk, understood the nature of sounds much better than Reis and that was one of the reasons why he was successful where Reis had failed. Bell, his father, and his grandfather were all teachers of speech and articulation. Bell had a school in Boston, Massachusetts, where he taught the deaf and those who had defective speech. Bell, the teacher, was naturally much interested in sounds and experimented constantly in search of new knowledge. It is said that he taught his dog to say, "How are you, Grandma?"

When Bell first started to experiment with electricity it was not to build a telephone. It was with the idea of making a telegraph

[1] The pitch of a sound is the highness or lowness of its tone.

instrument which would send out different musical sounds instead of dots and dashes for the different letters of the alphabet. By its use he hoped to send several telegraph messages at the same time over the same wire.

It was in 1875 that Bell took hold of the problem of building a telephone. He and his assistant, a young mechanic named Thomas A. Watson, Jr., had been working together for three years in the endeavor to perfect the musical telegraph. It was while experimenting with this "Harmonic Telegraph," as Bell called it, that he made a discovery that he thought could be used for building a speaking telephone. For nearly ten months, they toiled early and late to make an instrument which would carry speech. Finally, on March 10, 1876, they found what they had been looking for. Bell had run wires from his workshop at No. 5 Exeter Street, Boston, to his bedroom two floors away. He was at one end of the line and his assistant, Watson, was at the other. Bell spoke into his telephone and said, "Mr. Watson, come here; I want you." Watson, who was listening to the instrument at the other end of the line, understood the words and went.

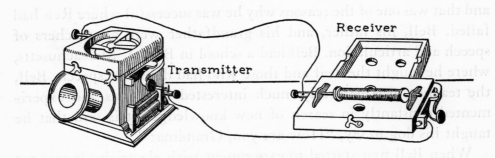

Receiver

Transmitter

THE REIS TELEPHONE INSTRUMENTS

Fifteen years before Bell made his first telephone, Johann Phillip Reis built a telephone from a coil of wire, the bung of a beer barrel, a knitting needle, sausage skin and a piece of platinum. The Reis telephone would transmit and reproduce music and certain sounds sent over wires connecting the transmitter and receiver but would not "talk" well. The sketch above was copied from a sketch in the instructions which accompanied the instruments built by Reis.

Just think, before that time it had never been possible to send the sound of the human voice any farther than a man could shout. Here now was a means of sending it many miles over wires. It would seem that everyone would have been very much excited over the new invention. But they weren't, at least no one except Bell and some of his closest friends. He had a hard time organizing a company and getting enough money to put his new idea on the market. That part of the problem was harder than making the original invention.

When Bell applied for a patent upon his new telephone, there occurred one of those strange coincidences sometimes met with in science. The world had been waiting a long time for a telephone to appear and then on the same day, February 14, 1876, two men applied for a patent on one. Both had invented similar contrivances. One man was Bell and the other Elisha Gray. It was decided that Bell's application had come into the United States Patent Office in Washington a few hours before Gray's and so Bell received the patent.

SWITCHBOARD OPERATOR

The telephone operator whose work it is to manipulate the switches, jacks, and plugs in a manually operated central office is gradually being replaced by automatic switching devices.

On October 9, 1876, Bell held the first recorded distant telephone conversation when he and Watson talked over a wire running between Cambridge and Boston. The first telephone company was organized in the summer of 1877. It is said that Bell's patent

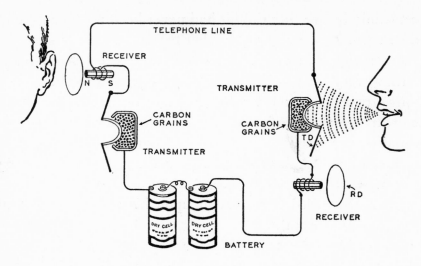

HOW DOES THE TELEPHONE OPERATE?

This is a circuit diagram showing two telephone receivers and two telephone transmitters connected in series with a battery. For simplicity, no call bells, switches, etc. are included. When one of the transmitters is spoken into (at right) the sounds cause the diaphragm (TD) to vibrate and shake up the carbon grains in the chamber attached to the diaphragm. The carbon grains vary their resistence to the current flowing in the line. The receiver consists of an iron diaphragm (RD) close to a permanent magnet (NS) and a coil of wire. The permanent magnet and the electromagnet (coil of wire) exert a pull on the iron diaphragm. The pull varies with the strength of the current flowing through the coil. Fluctuations in the current cause the diaphragm to vibrate and reproduce the sounds made at the transmitter.

was the most valuable single patent ever issued. There are now 74,000,000 telephones installed in the United States.

Bell's original telephone apparatus was of course very crude in comparison to the instruments now used. Strangest of all, it did not need any batteries—it generated its own electricity and the same instrument served as both the transmitter and the receiver.

The first Bell telephones which were installed for commercial service were really impractical. They buzzed and sputtered so that people regarded them as little more than interesting curiosities. In order to telephone, one had to shout at the top of his lungs and then quickly apply his ear to hear the faint voice coming from the other end of the line.

The Western Union Telegraph Company saw the faults of the Bell telephone and also the great possibilities. So it went into the telephone business and engaged Thomas A. Edison to develop a transmitter for them. Edison took up the work and devoted all of his genius to overcoming the difficulty which was preventing the telephone from coming into widespread use. He saw that a battery was necessary and in order to vary the battery current in accordance with the vibrations of the voice, he invented the carbon type telephone transmitter. He also devised the scheme of using an induction

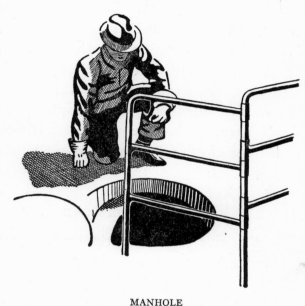

MANHOLE

Underground power lines and telephone and telegraph cables are reached through manholes.

coil in connection with the transmitter. The idea embraced in Edison's transmitter and coil is still the basis of the circuits of more than half the telephones in the world. He sold his patent to the Western Union Company for $100,000. Almost at once this improvement of Edison's put the telephone business on its feet. But it also started a commercial warfare between the Bell telephone and the Western Union interests. Later, these two rivals settled their difficulties and the American Speaking Telephone Company, owned by the Western Union Company, retired from the field.

In 1880, the American Bell Telephone Company was formed.

The telephone system which we know is the work of hundreds of men. It has been created step by step through thousands of small changes and improvements. No one who is not an old telephone engineer can appreciate all the possibilities of trouble that there are in a telephone system or realize all the problems that have been solved.

Alexander Graham Bell's great achievement was not so much the invention of the crude telephone instrument as it was his discovery and understanding of the principles and possibilities of using electric currents to carry conversations over wires for considerable distances.

The first telephone was a simple apparatus consisting of only a dozen parts. Today's telephone set is a vastly superior instrument consisting of over 450 precision-made parts.

TELEPHONE COMPANIES

Eighty-five per cent of the more than 74,000,000 telephones in this country are operated by Bell Telephone Companies and the other 15 per cent by some 3,300 independently owned telephone companies. The independent telephone industry was born with the expiration of Alexander Graham Bell's basic patents in 1894. Almon Brown Strowger, a Kansas City businessman, is credited with developing the first automatic telephone system (dial system). The first commercial application of Strowger's invention was in La Porte, Indiana, by an independent company.

HOW A TELEPHONE TRANSMITS SOUND

In order to understand how the telephone works, it is first necessary to understand something about sound.

The impression which the mind receives through the organ of hearing is called *sound*. Anything which produces sound *vibrates* and communicates its vibrations to the surrounding air so as to make waves in the air. When the sound waves strike anything which can move easily, especially a thin disk or membrane called a diaphragm, they cause the diaphragm to move exactly as the object did which produced the sound.

INSIDE A MANHOLE

This is the interior of a telephone manhole and shows the cables and racks and the iron **pots** containing loading coils.

The telephone is simply an instrument for sending sounds to a distant point by means of electric currents. The telephone transmitter of today is a sensitive electric ear. Fastened to the back of its eardrum (diaphragm) is a small chamber filled with a carefully measured quantity of carbon granules (grains of roasted coal). The carbon granules are part of the telephone circuit through which an electric current from a battery flows. The person who is using the telephone speaks into the diaphragm causing it to vibrate and move exactly as the eardrum (a diaphragm in our heads composed of membrane) does when it is struck by sound waves.

The vibrations of the diaphragm change the pressure of the carbon grains in the chamber. When the pressure on the carbon grains

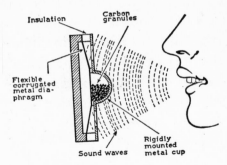

TRANSMITTER

The diaphragm in the telephone transmitter is set into motion by the sound waves of the voice.

decreases they offer a poor path to the electric current. As a consequence little current gets through.

When the pressure on the carbon grains is increased, they offer less resistance to the flow of electric current. As a result more current passes over the circuit. In that way the fluctuations of the diaphragm create corresponding fluctuations in the electric current passing through the transmitter.

One of the illustrations explains how the carbon grains control the current. The irregularly-shaped white objects in the sketches represent grains of carbon magnified about 30 times their normal size. D represents the diaphragm of the transmitter. The dotted lines represent the paths of electrons moving through the carbon grains. The streams of moving electrons are electric currents.

When no sounds reach the diaphragm, there is a steady flow of current through the circuit. A steady flow of current conveys no conversation.

But when sound waves strike the diaphragm, they cause it to move back and forth or vibrate, and vary the pressure of the carbon grains against one another. The carbon grains are then alternately in a loose condition and a small fraction of a second later are tightly packed together. This process repeats itself as long as the sound continues.

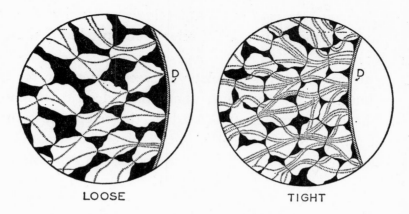

LOOSE   TIGHT

DIAGRAMS OF CARBON GRAINS (MAGNIFIED) IN A TRANSMITTER
WHICH EXPLAINS HOW SOUND VARIES THE TELEPHONE CURRENT

When the grains are under pressure and packed tightly together by the push of a sound wave moving the diaphragm inward, there are many more contacts (spots where the carbon grains touch one another) and consequently more paths for the electrons and less resistance in the path of the current. More current flows than when the grains are loose. Thus the vibrations of the diaphragm create exactly similar fluctuations in the current passing through the transmitter.

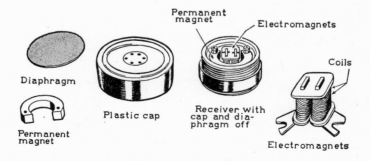

A TELEPHONE RECEIVER

This is the receiver unit from a handset used by one of the independent telephone companies.

The voice you hear coming from a telephone receiver is NOT the voice at the transmitter but is a similar sound produced *electrically* in the receiver.

There are several types of telephone receivers made for special purposes but they all transform fluctuating electric currents into sounds. The most common type used by the telephone companies consists of a thin iron disk (called the receiver diaphragm) which is placed near but not quite touching the poles of a small permanent magnet. The magnet exerts a pull on the iron diaphragm. Any change in the strength of the magnetic pull causes the diaphragm to move slightly.

A coil of fine insulated wire is wound around an iron core and attached to each pole of the magnet. The terminals of these coils are connected to wires leading from the transmitter and battery. The varying currents of electricity produced by vibrations of the transmitter diaphragm alternately increase and decrease the magnetism

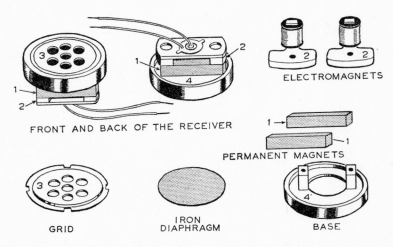

ELECTROMAGNETS

FRONT AND BACK OF THE RECEIVER

PERMANENT MAGNETS

GRID   IRON DIAPHRAGM   BASE

A TELEPHONE RECEIVER

This receiver unit differs slightly from the one in the preceding illustration but it operates in the same manner. Notice that two bar type permanent magnets are used instead of a single horseshoe magnet.

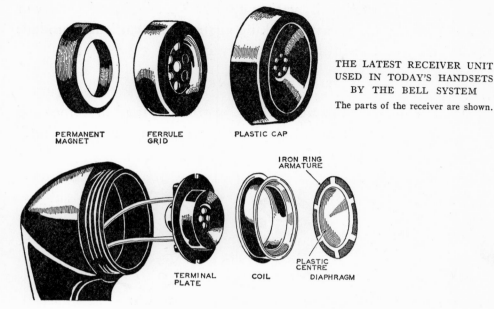

THE LATEST RECEIVER UNIT
USED IN TODAY'S HANDSETS
BY THE BELL SYSTEM
The parts of the receiver are shown.

PERMANENT
MAGNET

FERRULE
GRID

PLASTIC CAP

IRON RING
ARMATURE

TERMINAL
PLATE

COIL

PLASTIC
CENTRE

DIAPHRAGM

produced by the coils. These changes in the magnetic force pulling
on the diaphragm cause the diaphragm to vibrate. The vibrations
produce air waves and anyone listening at the receiver hears a replica
or imitation of the original words spoken into the transmitter.

The latest design of receiver unit used in the handsets of the Bell
Telephone Companies resembles a miniature radio loudspeaker more
than it does its predecessors. The flat iron disk which serves as the
diaphragm in receivers of an earlier design has been replaced by a
cone-shaped plastic diaphragm having an iron armature ring fastened to its edge. A circular coil placed inside a circular permanent
magnet forms the electromagnet which aids or opposes the pull of
the permanent magnet depending upon the flow of current through
the coil. The variation in magnetic pull causes the iron around the
edge of the diaphragm to move. The plastic cone or bowl-shaped
diaphragm moves back and forth with the iron ring at the same rate

and pushes against the air, setting up sound-producing air waves or vibrations. These air waves, striking against your eardrum, produce the sounds you hear in the telephone receiver.

THE TELEPHONE SET

The telephone companies call the instrument used in homes and offices to send and receive telephone messages a telephone "set."

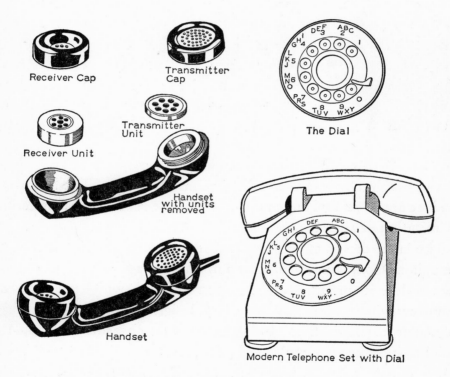

MODERN BELL SYSTEM TELEPHONE SET

The sketch in the lower right-hand corner shows the most widely used type of Bell System telephone set. Some of the independent telephone companies provide their customers with a set of similar appearance. The left-hand sketches shows details of today's Bell System handset. The transmitter and receiver units can be removed from the handle by unscrewing the plastic caps. If either unit becomes defective, a telephone repairman can replace it with a new unit in a few minutes.

Several changes of design have been made since 1940 but the principle of operation is the same for all types.

The modern telephone set consists of a handset and a steel and plastic base enclosing such auxiliary apparatus as a call bell or "ringer," a capacitor, induction coil and switches. If the set is equipped with a dial, the latter is mounted on the base and the gears and switches which the dial operates are enclosed within the base. The handset consists of a transmitter or microphone and a receiver mounted at opposite ends of a short plastic handle. When not in use, the handset is placed in a cradle fitted with a switch which operates automatically each time the handset is lifted up or replaced in the cradle. Some models of telephone sets are provided with a "hook" which serves the same purpose as the cradle. The hook moves a short distance when the handset is "hung up" or is lifted off. The movement of the hook automatically operates a switch within the telephone base.

TELEPHONE CENTRALS OR EXCHANGES

Since the telephone was invented for the purpose of enabling two people to talk to one another from a distance, it became necessary to provide some means by which telephones could be quickly and easily connected to one another. A number of different devices were tried but finally a completely equipped public telephone "exchange" was opened at New Haven, Connecticut, with a "switchboard" having a capacity of eight telephone lines. This was the first commercial telephone exchange and commenced operation on January 28, 1878. The telephone business, as we know it today, had taken its first step. Today switchboards located in central or exchange offices stand ready to connect your telephone quickly to any of the other millions of phones in the United States and some foreign countries.

SWITCHBOARDS

There are two kinds of switchboards in use: manual switchboards operated by hand and automatic switchboards operated by machines controlled from dial phones. In the manually operated exchanges, women telephone operators connect one telephone to another when a call is made and disconnect them when the call is finished.

Two wires from each subscriber's telephone terminate in a small socket called a telephone jack on a switchboard in the central office. There is a small electric light under each jack. When you wish to make a call and lift the receiver, it closes a switch and causes the light under your jack to flash. When the operator tending that switchboard sees the light, she pushes a plug into the jack connected to your phone. The plug is connected to a piece of flexible wire hav-

PLUG AND JACKS

The plugs and jacks of a manually-operated central switchboard are used to connect one telephone to another.

ing a similar plug at the other end. She also presses a switch which connects her receiver and transmitter to yours. She asks "number, please?" and if the jack connected to the phone bearing the number you request is on her switchboard, she pushes the second plug into it and presses the ringing key. This rings the bell at the phone which is being called. If the call is answered, lifting the receiver to answer disconnects the bell and connects

the receiver and transmitter to yours. Pulling out both plugs at the switchboard disconnects both phones.

MANUALLY OPERATED SWITCHBOARD AND OPERATOR

If a number is requested which is not on an operator's switchboard, she uses this same method to connect your phone with the switchboard where it is located. The operator there completes the call. Manual switchboards range in size from those handling only a

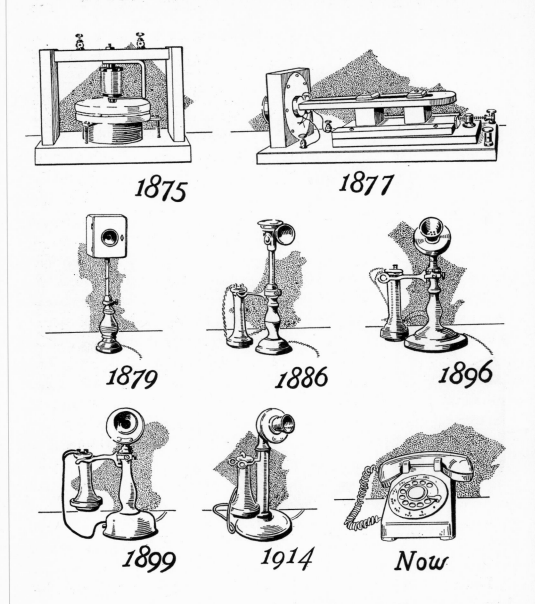

1875   1877

1879   1886   1896

1899   1914   Now

THE PROGRESS OF THE TELEPHONE INSTRUMENT

The telephone has gone through many changes since Bell made the original instrument (upper left) in 1875. Changes in central office equipment have been equally marked in the same period.

few telephones to big ones having as many as several thousand jacks within reach of the operator.

DIAL PHONES

An automatic switchboard connects your telephone to the one you wish without the assistance of a central operator. The phones connected to an automatic switchboard are equipped with dials. The dial is a calling device which you operate and control the switching machinery at the automatic switchboard. The visible part of the dial consists of a movable finger wheel with ten holes marked with the letters of the alphabet and the numerals 1, 2, 3, 4, 5, 6, 7, 8, 9, 0. Under the dial and enclosed within the base of the telephone is a switch. Turning the finger wheel and releasing it operates the switch. Each time the wheel is turned and released the switch opens and closes from one to ten times depending upon how far the wheel has been turned. Turning the finger wheel winds a spring so that when the wheel is released, the spring operates the switch. The switch is adjusted to send out current impulses at the rate of approximately 14 per second. If the first hole in the wheel is moved around to the stop and released, one current impulse is sent to the automatic switchboard. Moving the second finger hole around to the stop and releasing it sends out two current impulses and so on. The last hole, marked with zero and the word OPERATOR, if turned as far as the stop and released, causes ten current impulses to travel to the switchboard. The current impulses move relay switches on the switchboard. Turning the holes representing the various letters and numerals around against the stop in correct sequence so as to spell out a telephone number sends forth the proper number of current impulses to operate selector switches and connector switches at the automatic central and connects you with the telephone you desire.

Today more than nine out of ten Bell system telephones are dial telephones and are connected to central offices where automatic equipment performs the switching job.

HIGHWAYS FOR COMMUNICATION

Telephone and telegraph wires supported by poles alongside railroads and highways were once a familiar sight. The wires were bare but were insulated from the poles and cross arms by green glass insulators, very tempting targets for boys who liked to throw stones. The wires have been disappearing, being replaced by insulated wires formed into a cable and enclosed in a lead sheath. A cable $2\frac{5}{8}$ inches in diameter can replace 3,637 wires. (See Chapter Six.)

Many millions of miles of telephone wire spread throughout the U. S. to form our telephone network. The average person is not likely to see much of this because more and more wires are being placed in cables and the cables placed underground. About 98 per cent of all telephone wires in the Bell system are now in cables and 60 per cent of the cables are underground. All of the telephone traffic (conversations, television programs and data) over long distances between cities is usually in cables or handled by radio microwaves through the air. Many of the conductors in the cables and all of the microwaves used in telephony and telegraphy are "carriers" which handle large numbers of conversations simultaneously. (See Chapter Fourteen.)

Conversations and data travel with astounding speed over telephone lines but the currents carrying the spoken words and signals weaken rapidly as they travel along. Somewhere along the line, therefore, the currents must be given more energy. The device used to supply initial energy is the repeater or amplifier.

The telephone repeater is a three-electrode vacuum tube which operates as an amplifier. It strengthens and amplifies the feeble voice currents of the telephone line. Without repeaters there would be a limit of not more than 1,000 miles to long distance telephony. Voice currents travelling more than that distance would be so weakened and distorted that their message could not be understood. Consequently, long-distance messages pass through several repeater stations. There may be several hundred repeater stations used in a 2,500-mile conversation. Transmitter, repeater and receiver are the three basic elements of a long distance circuit.

CHAPTER NINE

ELECTRIC LIGHT

NOTHING which electricity does has added to your comfort and mine so much as the light wherewith to see after the sun disappears each night and darkness creeps upon us. We are so accustomed to electric lights that we never stop to think what the world would be like without any. This invention is believed by many scientists to be one of the world's greatest achievements. Before the year 1879, when the incandescent electric lamp was invented, the only lights the world had ever known burned with a flame. Every one of them depended upon consuming something—a fuel of some kind—and

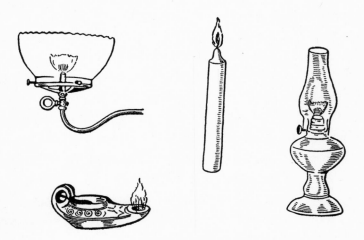

SOOT AND FLAME

From the time when faggots were burned to produce light and until the electric light was invented every form of lamp burned with a flame and consumed carbon. The incandescent electric lamp was the first light to burn without flame or soot and it consumed electricity, not carbon.

THOMAS A. EDISON EXPERIMENTING WITH CARBON FILAMENTS
This sketch was redrawn from an illustration in *Harper's Weekly* of 1880.

the fuel was almost always carbon. No matter whether the light came from a gas jet, an oil lamp burning whale oil or kerosene, a candle, a pine knot or an arc lamp, a flame was always there. A supply of fuel had to be kept up or the light would go out. The light also required oxygen. This it took from the surrounding air and gave back in return particles of soot, heat, smoke, and "bad air."

A young man, who was only thirty-two years of age at the time, perfected the incandescent electric lamp. If you don't know who it was, you should. It was Thomas Alva Edison. In 1878 the former newsboy and telegraph operator, who was becoming famous all over the world for his inventions, commenced his endeavors to produce a perfect electric incandescent lamp that would be capable of replacing gas and oil for lighting buildings, homes and streets.

THE FIRST ELECTRIC LIGHT

The only electric lights in existence at that time were called "arcs." They were suitable for lighting streets, large stores and halls but not homes. They were huge affairs, they gave too much light, used too much current and sputtered and flickered. The arc was really an electric fire fed with fuel made of carbon rods. It was discovered by Humphry Davy in 1800. At that time Sir Humphry Davy was already a well-known scientist. He was born in Cornwall, England, in 1778. His father was a poor woodcarver. Young Davy received a grammar-school education and then, upon the death of his father, was apprenticed to a surgeon. The young scientist was only twenty-one years old when he

ELECTRIC ARC

The form of lamp once used for street lighting and now for artificial sun bathing. The sketch shows how the electric arc between two carbon rods would appear if you looked at it through smoked glass.

discovered that a gas called *nitrous oxide* could be inhaled with no bad after-effects. Nitrous oxide is the gas which dentists now use as an anaesthetic for pulling teeth.

When the young scientist heard about Volta's new "pile," he made one and discovered that it would make electric sparks when two wires connected to its terminals were rubbed together. He also found that if two pieces of charcoal were connected with the wires, the sparks would become much brighter. Davy tucked this information away in his head for future use.

The miners' safety-lamp was invented by Davy. Prior to this invention, many mine explosions were caused by the open-flame lamps which miners used. The flame in a Davy lamp is surrounded by a fine wire screen and gives warning of explosive gases.

When Davy was twenty-three years old he became a lecturer at the Royal Institution in London. Now he had everything he might wish for to experiment with. Remembering his old experiments with the feeble voltaic pile, he connected two pieces of charcoal to a powerful battery of 150 cells and brought them into contact for a moment. When he drew them apart a dazzling, brilliant light astonished the scientist. This was the first electric light.

A Frenchman named Foucault found that the arc could be much improved by using pencils of hard carbon instead of the sticks of charcoal Davy had employed. The arc was then gradually developed until it became very useful for lighting outdoor places and large interiors.

A man named Charles F. Brush, and the men associated with him, made the arc practical for lighting purposes. They made it self-adjusting and also developed suitable dynamos for generating the necessary current. The first electric lights to be permanently installed for illuminating a public street were twelve 2,000-candle-power Brush arc lamps set up on ornamental poles in Public Square, Cleveland, Ohio, in 1879. Imagine what a wonder these were to people who had been accustomed to oil lamps and candles. Today almost the only chance you will have to see an arc lamp (unless you make one yourself) is in the form of one of the old-fashioned therapeutic lamps used to generate ultra-violet rays as a substitute for those of the sun in the wintertime.

The rays from a carbon arc are of great value in curing certain skin diseases and for treating or "irradiating" foods, as it is called, so as to provide vitamin D.

A NEW LIGHT SHINES

When Edison set to work to develop a new type of electric light, he realized that in order to be successful he would have to make a much smaller lamp than the arc. As he put it in his own words, what he intended to do was "subdivide the electric current." What did "subdivide" mean? It meant that with the same current used to light a single arc-lamp, he intended to light a number of small units—lights of about the same candle power as the flame of illuminating gas from the old-fashioned gas-jet.

THE FIRST PRAC-
TICAL CARBON
FILAMENT LAMP

The filament was made from a piece of cotton thread.

As early as 1841, Frederick de Moleyns, an Englishman, had tried to build a small electric lamp. He enclosed a metal wire in a glass bulb from which he had exhausted most of the air. Others made similar attempts. In 1860 Joseph W. Swan devised a lamp made of a strip of carbonized paper and the same year, or perhaps a year earlier, Moses G. Farmer used platinum and iridium wires in lamps connected to primary batteries. None of these experimenters accomplished anything practical.

Edison started where they had left off and went to work along the same lines, making use of the fact that heat is generated by a current of electricity. When an electric current passes through a wire under the proper conditions enough heat may be produced to make the wire white hot so that it glows with a brilliant light. It requires considerable current to heat a large wire or conductor, and so Edison's first problem was to find a substance that could be formed into a fine hair-like filament and which would not melt when it became incandescent. He experimented with platinum because it has a very high melting point. His earliest lamps consisted of a spiral of very thin platinum wire sealed in a small glass bulb from which the air had been exhausted. An electric current passing through the platinum wire heated it almost white hot or incandescent, which means "glowing with heat"—whence came the name of the lamp. Since every substance requires oxygen in order to burn, and all the air containing oxygen was pumped out of the glass bulb, the platinum could not burn. But it was unsatisfactory. It had to be brought so near its melting point in order to give a good light that a very small increase in the electric current would destroy it. He tried platinum alloyed with the rare metal iridium. It was unsuccessful,

LIGHT FIXTURES

These early electric-light fixtures resemble the gas lights at the time. The sketches were redrawn from an illustration in *Harper's Weekly* of 1880.

as were further experiments with silicon, boron, and a host of other materials. Edison was convinced that he was on the wrong track. Thirteen months of tireless investigation had passed without bringing any encouragement. Platinum and all other metals were abandoned. Edison started experimenting with the material which men had been burning to produce light ever since they had known how to

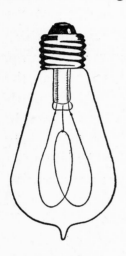

CARBON FILA-
MENT LAMP

This type of lamp, once in universal use, has been replaced by the more efficient tungsten filament lamp.

light a fire—nothing more or less than carbon. He made filaments of tar and lampblack. A good light was the result, but it did not last. The filament burned out. Carbon seemed to be the right thing but not when made of a mixture of lampblack and tar. He sent out and bought a spool of cotton thread, bent a piece of the thread into a loop, shaped like a hairpin, turned the thread into carbon by baking it and sealed it in a bulb. It was a nerve-racking battle to obtain one single piece of hairpin-shaped carbonized thread that would not break before it could be sealed in a lamp. For two and one-half days Edison and his assistants worked without sleep. Success came on October 21, 1879. Current was turned on the first lamp with a carbon filament made from a cotton thread. A beautiful soft glow came from the lamp. It burned forty-five hours. This was the first encouragement in all the long months of disappointment. It had shown that carbon would glow for a long time at a temperature at which platinum would quickly melt. Thereupon Edison and his men started the greatest filament making and carbonizing "bee" on record. Just about everything that you can think of was tried. Of all the substances tested during this period paper seemed the most likely and Edison started the regular manufacture

of lamps with looped filaments of carbonized paper. These were put
into service within the laboratory, in nearby dwellings and along the
neighborhood roads.

FOR A LONG TIME ALL INCANDESCENT LAMPS HAD
CARBON FILAMENTS

But if the cotton-thread lamp had not satisfied its inventor, neither
did the paper filament lamp, in spite of its comparative success.
Edison kept his large corps of men continually prospecting for something better.

In the laboratory one day in the early part of 1880, Edison picked
up an ordinary palm-leaf fan. He saw that the edge was bound with
a long, flexible strip of bamboo. He tore it off and gave it to one of
his assistants with directions to split it into pieces suitable for carbonizing into filaments. When tried, these filaments proved much
superior to anything else which had been found up to that time.

The Chinese and Japanese have long used bamboo for every con-
ceivable purpose. Furniture, houses, food, weapons, paper, musical
instruments, hats, and boats are just a few of its uses. A servant of
man from primitive ages, this marvellous vegetable now became an
adjunct to modern electrical science.

So it was with a bamboo filament that the incandescent lamp was
established and won its early triumphs. Indeed as late as 1898 it was
still employed for making lamps of certain designs. (See note at end
of this chapter.)

THE FIRST METAL FILAMENT LAMPS

But scientists and engineers never seem to be satisfied and there
was something about the idea of a filament made out of metal in-

stead of carbon which especially appealed to them. So they kept looking. Finally in 1903, Doctor Auer von Welsbach, the German scientist who was the inventor of the incandescent gas mantle, produced an electric lamp having a filament made of the rare metal called osmium. Osmium is a very hard metal which is a sort of half-brother to platinum and iridium. It is seldom used for anything except the tips of fountain pens. Welsbach's new filament proved to be much more efficient than carbon. It would produce a whiter light and more of it in return for the same amount of current. It was not long before the osmium filament was followed by one invented in the research laboratories of the great German firm of Siemens and Halske in which the metal tantalum was used.

Carbon, osmium and tantalum have been replaced by tungsten. Tungsten filament lamps were first produced commercially in America in 1907. This was the beginning of a revolution in the methods of manufacturing incandescent lamps. Thereafter American lamp manufacturers assumed the lead in developing and improving the lamp.

As a result of research at the General Electric Company on an old idea introduced in 1878 by W. E. Sawyer and A. Man, it was found that an inert gas within the bulb of a tungsten lamp, instead of a vacuum, greatly increases the efficiency. By an inert gas is meant one in which tungsten will not burn. A mixture containing 86 per cent argon and 14 per cent nitrogen is generally used in the manufacture of gas-filled lamps of the best quality.

THE FIRST ELECTRIC LIGHT PLANTS

Edison did a great deal more than simply perfect the process of making an incandescent lamp. He had to build suitable dynamos for supplying the current, meters for measuring it, sockets for hold-

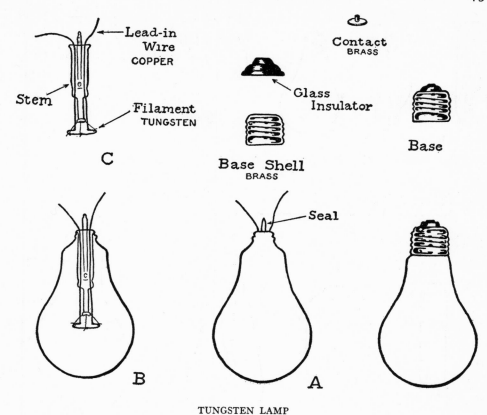

TUNGSTEN LAMP

You cannot see inside a common electric-light bulb used for house lighting because the glass is frosted or partially opaque. Frosting overcomes the bright glare of the filament and diffuses or spreads the light more evenly. *A* shows a bulb with the base removed. *B* shows how the stem and filament are mounted inside the bulb.

ing the lamps, switches, fuses, and everything necessary for a complete lighting system. Outside of the boilers and steam-engines for driving the generators, the Edison organization had to originate every component part.

The world's first commercial central station for incandescent lighting was that installed on Holborn Viaduct in London, England, by the English Edison Electric Light Company. The switch which put the plant into service was closed on January 12, 1882.

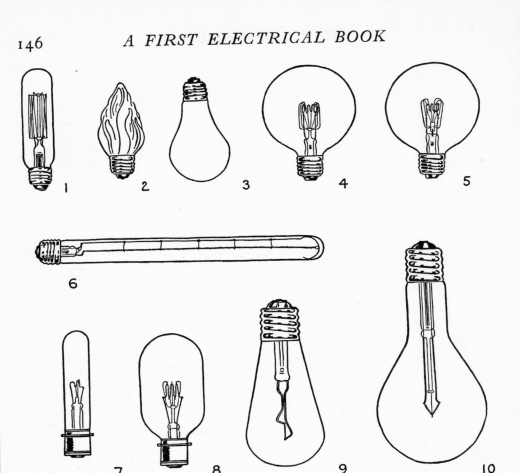

THE SAME IN PRINCIPLE

All of these lamps are the same in principle—a tungsten filament inside a gas-filled bulb—but each has been designed for some particular purpose. Numbers 1, 7, and 8 are projection lamps for moving-picture machines. Number 2 is a decorative lamp made to resemble the flame of a torch. Number 3 is the type used for general lighting. Number 4 is especially designed for spotlights and number 5 is a floodlight lamp. Number 6 is a showcase lamp. Numbers 9 and 10 are street-lighting lamps.

The first station to be built in the United States was at 255–257 Pearl Street, New York City. It went into operation generating electric current for about 400 incandescent lamps scattered around the neighborhood at three o'clock in the afternoon on September 4, 1882. The station continued in use until 1895.

HOW LAMPS ARE MANUFACTURED

All the incandescent lamps made for house lighting now have "frosted" bulbs to diffuse the light and eliminate the concentrated glare of the filament. The first frosted lamps were etched on the outside of the bulb. Now they are frosted inside so as not to gather dirt.

At one time there were hundreds of small lamp manufacturers in this country but now the General Electric and Westinghouse Lamp Companies have an almost complete monopoly of the business. Concentrating manufacture in a few large plants made it possible to do research and development work which has greatly improved the lamps and at the same time reduced their price.

Making an incandescent lamp was once the work of skilled lampmakers. Now it is done almost entirely by machinery. Some of the machines are entirely automatic—others merely require the guidance or control of hands. The bulbs for certain sizes of lamps are made by automatic machines which work twenty-four hours a day.

THE DIFFERENT KINDS OF LAMPS

A tungsten lamp is really a simple thing. As we have seen, the light is produced by heating

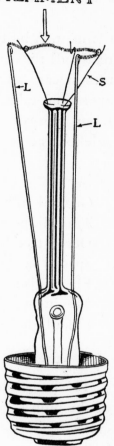

FILAMENT

WHERE DOES THE LIGHT COME FROM?

The filament is the light-producer in an incandescent lamp. The filament of a modern lamp is a tungsten wire wound in a fine spring. The wires marked *L* conduct the current to the filament. The fine wires marked *S* aid in supporting the filament.

a thin metal filament to incandescence, the heat being produced by the current forcing its way through the great resistance of the filament. A bulb, a filament, and a base for connecting the lamp are really all that are necessary. But these parts must be made with the utmost care and accuracy. A great many different manufacturing operations take place on each one. And there are a great many different types of lamps, each one especially made so as to be most suitable for a certain purpose. Here is a partial list of the different kinds.

General lighting

Street lighting

Train lighting

Sign lighting

Decorative lighting

Automobile lighting

Special lamps are made for

Flashlights

Airway beacons

Moving-picture projectors

Showcases

Floodlights

Medical instruments

The principle used in all of these is the same. The size and shape of the bulb varies and so does the filament. The smallest lamps are called "grains of wheat" and are smaller than the smallest flashlight bulbs. They are used by doctors in surgical instruments. The largest have bulbs more than a foot in diameter and develop up to 100,000 candle power. They are made for use in moving-picture studios and it is claimed that the light from them is the nearest approach yet obtained to sunlight. The filament used in the largest lamps is a ribbon of tungsten. That in the lamps used for house lighting is a wire coiled up into such a tiny spring that it looks like a plain wire. It is necessary to magnify the filament considerably before it can be seen that it is a spring.

PHOTOFLASH LAMPS

These lamps, first introduced in 1930, revolutionized photography. Although they have the appearance of incandescent lamps, they do not operate on the same principle. They are "combustion" lamps. Their burning life is only a few hundredths of a second and they can be used once only. Instead of burning waxes or oils as in the historical candle and oil lamp, photoflash lamps burn aluminum foil or wire. Aluminum is used because it burns easily and produces an intense white light. The glass lamp bulb is merely a container for the inflammable metal and pure oxygen. The small filament in the bulb serves simply as a match which ignites the aluminum. The inner and outer surfaces of a photoflash bulb are coated with clear lacquer to prevent the glass from scattering if it should be shattered.

VAPOR LAMPS

About the time Benjamin Franklin performed his famous experiment with a kite and proved that lightning is an electrical discharge, an English scientist discovered something important that electricity will do. This scientist, an apothecary and member of the Royal Society named Thomas Watson, discovered that light is produced when electricity passes through a partial vacuum. Dr. Watson pumped some of the air from a glass tube about three feet long and then sent a charge from a Leyden jar through the tube. He was greatly pleased with what he saw. For a split second, the tube was filled with a soft glow. "It was," he wrote, "a most delightful spectacle when the room was darkened to see the electricity in its passage."

At the time of Watson's discovery, an electric current was unknown. Volta had not yet invented the Voltaic pile or the Voltaic cell. Scientists could use only static electricity in their experiments. The discharge of a Leyden jar is miniature lightning and like lightning it is gone in a jiffy. The light produced by Watson's tube was consequently only a flash. No one knew how to make it continuous and steady.

Two centuries later, we use lamps which employ the same principle as Watson's tube. Now we have the knowledge and the means to make tubular "vapor" lamps which glow continuously and steadily. They are replacing incandescent filament lamps for many purposes. Their light is produced by sending a current of electricity through rarefied gas or vapor. They glow steadily because they utilize a current of electricity, not a static charge as Watson's tube did.

NEON LAMPS

A vapor lamp with which the whole world is familiar is the neon lamp used for signs and advertising. Neon sign lamps consist of long glass tubes exhausted of all but a tiny amount of their air and containing a small amount of the rare gas called neon. The tube may be straight or bent into any shape. A metal electrode is sealed in each end of the tube. The electrodes are connected to a transformer which increases 120-volt current to several thousand volts. When the high-voltage current passes through the rarefied gas in the tube, the tube glows. The presence of neon causes it to glow more brightly than it would without neon. If neon alone is used, the light which is produced contains no blue rays and is of a striking red color. By introducing a small amount of mercury into the tube, the color of the light is changed from red to blue. When the tube is made of uranium glass and contains both neon and mercury, the light is green. By the use of other combinations of gases, vapors and glass, twelve different colors can be obtained.

MERCURY ARC LAMPS

The ghostly greenish-blue light which comes from within some mills and factories is usually produced by an arc. If the light flickers and varies, it is made by an arc used for welding. If the light is steady it is probably produced by a mercury arc lamp.

Human vision is much sharper in the light from a mercury arc lamp than it is in the light from other types of lamps. For that reason, mercury arcs are used for illumination where precision manufacturing and inspection are carried on. Mercury arc lamps are to be found in many photographic studios, in printing plants, in tool rooms and in mills where fine textured fabrics are woven.

One of the earliest commercial mercury arc lamps was invented by P. Cooper Hewitt in 1901. Hewitt's lamp consists of a long glass tube containing mercury but exhausted of air. An electrode was sealed in each end of the tube. The Cooper Hewitt arc lamps were lighted by tilting the tube so that the mercury ran back and forth. Later, they were improved so that they started automatically. Cooper

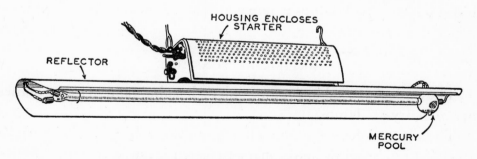

A COOPER HEWITT MERCURY–VAPOR ARC LAMP

One of the earliest mercury-vapor light sources and formerly widely used in industrial lighting. The principal use today for this type of lamp is for photography, photostat and similar photocopy work.

Hewitt lamps are still encountered in industrial lighting, but their principal use today is for photography, photostat and similar photocopy work.

The most widely used mercury arc lamp is the 400-watt lamp known as type H–1. It is a tubular lamp about 13 inches long and 2 inches in diameter. It has a mogul base so that it can be screwed into a socket like an ordinary incandescent lamp. Inside the lamp are two tungsten main electrodes, a small quantity of mercury, a small amount of pure argon gas and a tube called the arc tube. The electrodes are at opposite ends of the arc tube. The lamp must be operated in a vertical position. When current is turned on a bluish glow fills the entire arc tube for about two minutes.

Then as the tube warms and the mercury is vaporized, the glow fades. In about 7 minutes after starting, the arc is a pencil-like stream of electrons which gives forth a very intense light. Although the light source appears to be bluish-white, there is an absence of red in it. Most colored objects are distorted in color value in the light from a mercury arc. Blue, green and yellow colors in objects are emphasized while orange and red appear brownish or black. A human face is given a ghastly appearance, the lips appear blue and the skin has a greenish hue. For that reason mercury lamps are often combined with filament lamps where good color appearance is important.

ARTIFICIAL SUNSHINE

The sunlamps used in doctors' offices, hospitals and in many homes are mercury arc lamps.

The ultra-violet rays so necessary to good health are missing from the light produced by an ordinary tungsten incandescent lamp. Several varieties of "sunlamp" have been developed to supply artificial

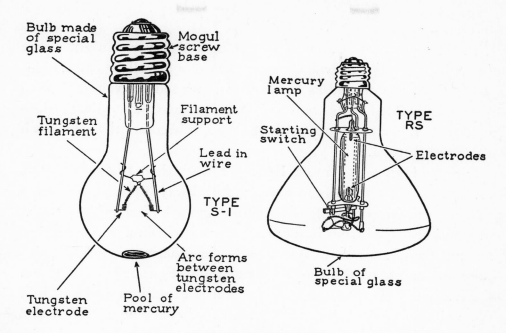

Bulb made of special glass

Mogul screw base

Tungsten filament

Filament support

Lead in wire

TYPE S-1

Tungsten electrode

Pool of mercury

Arc forms between tungsten electrodes

Mercury lamp

Starting switch

TYPE RS

Electrodes

Bulb of special glass

ARTIFICIAL SUNSHINE

Sunlamps furnish the ultra-violet radiation which is present in sunlight but not in the light from filament lamps. The Type S-1 sunlamp is a combination filament lamp and mercury arc. It is used where ultra-violet radiation and visible light are both desired. Type S-1 lamps will not operate on ordinary lighting circuits and will not fit ordinary sockets.

The Type RS sunlamp is designed for home use. It can be operated on ordinary lighting circuits. The filament in this type of lamp is not designed to produce light. It is a source of heat for starting the lamp and a ballast resistance which prevents too much current from flowing through the arc.

sunshine. Two "sunlamps" are illustrated. Both consist of a glass bulb enclosing a drop of mercury, a tungsten filament and two tungsten electrodes. When the filament is lighted, its heat vaporizes the mercury and the current then arcs between the two electrodes. The glowing mercury vapor produces visual light and also sufficient ultra-violet to produce a mild sunburn in five to ten minutes on un-tanned skin.

SODIUM LAMPS

Perhaps you may have travelled along a highway at night where the light from the overhead lamps had a soft yellow color. This yellow light is produced by lamps filled with sodium vapor. Sodium is a silver colored metal which is soft and waxy at ordinary temperatures. When combined with chlorine, it becomes the salt which we use in our food.

Sodium lamps give more light per watt than filament lamps. They are used principally in street and highway lighting. The 145-watt sodium lamp consists of a tubular inner bulb about 12 inches long and about 3 inches in diameter placed within a double-walled vacuum flask. This arrangement is like a Thermos bottle in principle; it maintains the tubular inner bulb at proper temperature.

The inner bulb contains a small quantity of sodium and neon gas. The neon aids in starting the lamp. Coiled filaments at either end serve as cathodes. (A cathode is the negative pole or electrode of an electrolytic cell or tube.) One side of each filament is connected to

10,000 LUMEN SODIUM LAMP FOR STREET AND HIGHWAY LIGHTING
In this sketch the outer glass bulb of the lamp is cut away to show its double wall.

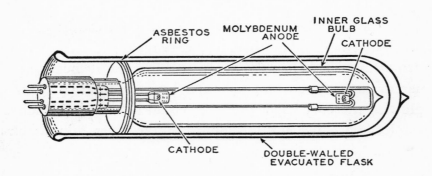

ASBESTOS RING   MOLYBDENUM ANODE   INNER GLASS BULB   CATHODE

CATHODE   DOUBLE-WALLED EVACUATED FLASK

a molybdenum anode. (An anode is the positive pole or electrode of an electrolytic cell or tube.) Molybdenum is a metal which is indispensable for the grids and screens of some varieties of radio tubes. The filaments which form the cathodes of a sodium lamp do not produce any illumination. They are used to start the lamp. When current is turned on, at first the neon gas glows with its characteristic red color. Then as the temperature rises, the sodium evaporates and the sodium vapor begins to glow. It requires about 30 minutes for the sodium vapor to reach its full brilliancy and normal color.

FLUORESCENT LAMPS

Fluorescent lamp is the popular name for a type of lamp which electrical engineers call an electric discharge lamp. It consists of a

FLUORESCENT LAMP

There are three types of fluorescent lamps in general use. The "General" type is illustrated above. It has two contact pins on each end which fit into a special socket. A special starter is necessary for starting the lamp.

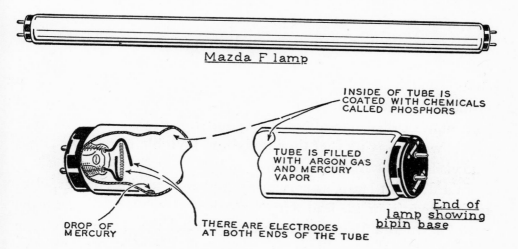

Mazda F lamp

INSIDE OF TUBE IS COATED WITH CHEMICALS CALLED PHOSPHORS

TUBE IS FILLED WITH ARGON GAS AND MERCURY VAPOR

End of lamp showing bipin base

DROP OF MERCURY

THERE ARE ELECTRODES AT BOTH ENDS OF THE TUBE

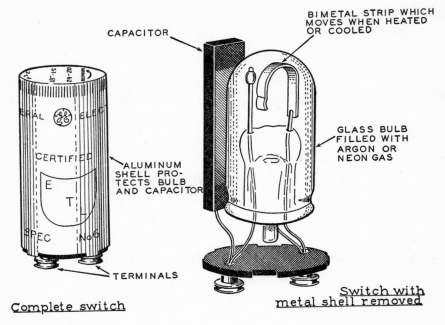

CAPACITOR

BIMETAL STRIP WHICH
MOVES WHEN HEATED
OR COOLED

GLASS BULB
FILLED WITH
ARGON OR
NEON GAS

ALUMINUM
SHELL PRO-
TECTS BULB
AND CAPACITOR

TERMINALS

Complete switch

Switch with
metal shell removed

STARTER FOR GENERAL TYPE FLUORESCENT LAMP

When current is turned on a General type lamp, no current flows for an instant except a
small amount producing a glow in the argon between the electrodes in the starter. This glow
heats the bimetal strip causing it to move and start the lamp.

tubular glass bulb containing a small drop of mercury and a small
amount of argon gas. The argon aids in starting the electrical discharge which flows through the mercury vapor in the tube. The
inside wall of the glass tube is coated with a mixture of chemical
compounds called phosphors. Phosphors fluoresce. That is the scientific way of saying that they transform invisible ultra-violet light
into visible light of various colors.

In a filament lamp, as previously explained in this chapter, electricity flows from one lead wire to another, through a solid tungsten
wire known as a filament. In an electric discharge lamp there is an
electrode sealed in each end of the tube. The electrodes are sep-

arated from each other with no apparent connection between them. Electricity flows from one to the other either through a vacuum, a gas, or a vapor. In the familiar fluorescent lamp, the electricity flows from one electrode to the other through mercury vapor. Very little visible light is produced by the flow of current through the mercury vapor. However, a great deal of ultra-violet radiation results and this causes the phosphor coating on the inside of the tube to glow and give forth soft light characteristic of fluorescent lamps.

NOTE

Lamps with filaments made of carbonized bamboo were replaced by lamps with "squirted" carbon filaments. Squirted filaments were made by dissolving cotton in a chemical solution and squirting this mixture through a die into alcohol to harden it. The thread-like filament thus formed was then carbonized by heating it. Lamps with "squirted" carbon filaments were in use for many years until replaced by lamps with tantalum and tungsten filaments.

CHAPTER TEN

HOW ELECTRICITY IS GENERATED AND THE ELECTRIC MOTOR DOES ITS WORK

WE would not be using electricity to light our homes, drive electric motors or do a great many other things requiring much power if the dynamo had not been invented. The electricity developed by batteries would be too expensive for most ordinary purposes. It is often said that we are living in an electrical age because we use electricity in so many ways. It is the dynamo which made this possible.

There is no more impressive or fascinating place than a large power house. Although electric current of tremendous power is being generated, there is nothing of it to be seen. There is something mysterious about the huge dynamos (also called generators),

THE BURLINGTON ZEPHYR

This was one of the first high-speed, lightweight, streamlined trains whose power plants are a combination of a Diesel engine and electric generator.

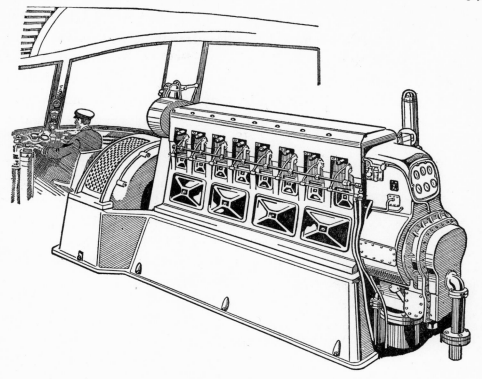

POWER PLANT

The power plant of the Burlington Zephyr consists of a large Diesel engine driving a dynamo
or generator. Current from the generator drives electric motors geared to the wheels.

revolving at high speed day and night. They whirl around incessantly, transforming the energy of huge steam engines, steam or water turbines into the invisible electric current that goes travelling out through cities and country over a huge network of copper wires. Men have learned how to build these huge generators so that they are almost perfect. They have been built to develop more than 275,-000 horsepower in a single machine. When properly cared for they give almost no trouble. A modern dynamo is the creation of thousands of men, but one man made the first one. It was more than one hundred years ago, in 1831 to be exact, when the first machine, other than a battery, was made for producing a current of electricity. The name of the man who did this has already been mentioned. He was Michael Faraday—probably the greatest experimenter that ever lived. Some day when you know more about electricity than you do now, go to a library and get a biography of this famous man. An account of his life and scientific work is very interesting.

MICHAEL FARADAY

He was the world's greatest experimenter. He discovered induction, invented the dynamo and made many valuable contributions to electrical science.

Michael Faraday was born September 22, 1791, in a small village near London, England. His father was a blacksmith named James Faraday who died after a long illness when Michael was nineteen years old. Michael had a chance to get only the most rudimentary education and had to assist his mother in providing for the family. He went to work as an errand boy to a bookbinder and stationer when he was thirteen years old. He performed his work so carefully that the following year his employer took him as an apprentice to learn the art of bookbinding.

During the years while he was an apprentice, young Faraday made good use of his time by reading some of the books which came into the shop. He was particularly interested in any book which told him something about science. He made several simple pieces of electrical apparatus and performed simple electrical and chemical experiments. Aside from his own reading and the things he thus taught himself, this young man had no scientific education other than a dozen lectures by a Mr. Tatum on natural philosophy and four lectures on chemistry by Sir Humphry Davy. Yet he earned for himself one of the greatest names in science.

The neat, carefully written notes of Sir Humphry's lectures which Faraday made and bound himself, served him a very useful purpose when he finished his apprenticeship. Faraday knew that he would not be happy as a bookbinder, so he applied to Sir Humphry Davy for a position, however menial, at the Royal Institution of which Davy was then director. With his application, Faraday sent along the notes he had taken of Davy's four lectures "as proof of his earnestness." It has been said that although Davy made a great many remarkable scientific discoveries, his greatest discovery was Michael Faraday. Davy was so pleased with the letter and the notes

DISAPPEARING AND ABOUT GONE

The first trolley cars were built in the 1880's. The development of the dynamo and the electric motor made them possible. Trolley cars were once an important part of America's transportation system. Motor buses have replaced them.

that Faraday was engaged as apparatus and lecture assistant at 25 shillings per week. He was not quite twenty-one years of age at the time.

For nearly fifty years Faraday labored at the Royal Institution, performing thousands of experiments and making discoveries which earned him the name of "father of electrical science." When he was thirty-four years old he was made Director of the Laboratory. Perhaps the secret of his success, which brought him honors from all over the scientific world and immortalized his name, may be found in some of the ideas which he left in his many notebooks. Faraday's advice was always:

"Aim at high things but not presumptuously.

Endeavor to succeed—expect not to succeed.

EDISON DYNAMO

This is the machine designed and used by Edison in his first electric-light plants. He also used one of these generators as a motor in his experiments with electric railways.

Never make a fact your own without seeing it."

In appearance, of course, the first dynamo was not anything like the machines made to-day. It was merely a piece of laboratory apparatus made to prove an idea. In one of Faraday's notebooks, which are still preserved in the Royal Institution, he wrote a reminder for a future experiment to "change magnetism into electricity." He

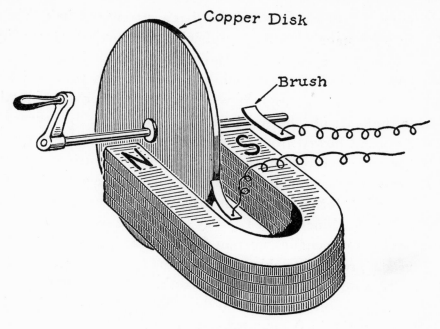

FARADAY'S GENERATOR

The huge generators which supply electric current for lighting a whole countryside had their beginning in this simple affair devised by the famous Michael Faraday.

thought about this problem a great deal. He even carried a magnet and a coil wire around in his pocket to think and ponder over.

What Faraday finally did was reverse Oersted's experiment which you read about on the first page of Chapter Four. He found that if a magnet is moved toward or away from a coil of wire, or if the wire is moved toward or away from a magnet, a momentary electric current is induced in the wire.

This experiment was really of much more importance to science than it may seem at first. Not only did it definitely connect the ancient lodestone with the electric current of Volta's batteries, but it also showed that there is a close relationship between electricity, magnetism, and motion.

Faraday could not help but notice that a current was induced only as long as the magnet or the coil of wire was moving. He realized that in order to obtain a continuous current, the motion must also be continuous, so he devised a machine to accomplish this. This machine was the first dynamo. It was simply a copper disk, rotating between the poles of a horseshoe magnet. When the disk turned an electric current flowed from the shaft to the rim or vice versa, according to which direction the disk turned. The current was conducted from the machine by means of two wires, one pressing against the shaft and the other against the disk.

The little machine which Faraday built more than a century ago could not generate enough current for any practical purpose. It had to undergo a great many changes to become useful. The first change was to substitute a coil of wire for the disk.

The simplest form of practical dynamo is a coil of wire (called the armature winding) mounted on a shaft and arranged to revolve between the poles of a magnet (called the field magnet). Two in-

THE SIMPLEST FORM OF ALTERNATING–CURRENT GENERATOR

This machine would produce an alternating current. There is little difference between an alternating-current generator and one delivering direct current. The alternating makes use of collector rings and the direct-current generator employs a commutator to lead the current out of the armature.

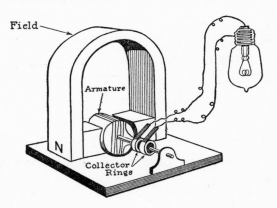

sulated rings (called collector rings) are mounted on the shaft and each connected to one end of the revolving armature coil. A little strip of thin copper or copper gauze (called the brushes) presses against each ring. The rings and the brushes lead the current out from the armature so that it may be employed for some useful work such as lighting a lamp.

In a dynamo of this sort, the current which is generated reverses its direction every half revolution of the armature. Such a current is called an alternating current (abbreviated AC) and the dynamo or generator which produces it is called an alternator.

By providing more than one field magnet so that the coil rotates between more than one set of poles, the currents may be made to flow backwards and forwards several times during each revolution of the armature. One complete flow of current backwards and forwards is called a *cycle* and the number of cycles per second is known as the frequency. The current ordinarily supplied for houselighting has a frequency of sixty cycles, which means that it flows back and

THE SIMPLEST FORM OF DIRECT–CURRENT GENERATOR

All generators develop alternating current but by use of a commutator mounted on the shaft the current actually delivered may be changed to direct.

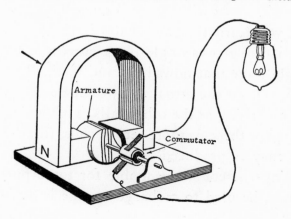

TELEPHONE MAGNETO

The telephone magneto is a small hand-operated generator which produces alternating
current and is still used in some telephone systems for ringing or calling.

forth sixty times per second. You have no doubt heard of "60 cycle"
current and now you know what it is.

Another term which is often used in speaking of alternating current is the word "phase." Perhaps you have heard of "single-phase,
two-phase, and three-phase" current. You will understand that better also when you learn that a dynamo having one coil or set of
coils on the armature gives a single-phase current—that is, a current
that has a single wave that flows back and forth. By arranging two
distinct sets of coils on the armature two separate waves of current
are produced, one rising as the other falls. This is a two-phase current. By employing three or more sets of coils, three-phase or polyphase currents may be produced.

An alternating current is unsuitable for some purposes, it cannot, for instance, be used to recharge storage batteries, to electro-

plate or in many chemical processes. So dynamos are often arranged to produce a continuous or direct current which is like the current from a battery. It flows only in one direction. This is very easily accomplished by making a change in the arrangement for collecting or leading out the current from the armature coil. In place of two rings, a single ring divided into two parts, each part being connected to one end of the coil, is mounted on the shaft. This arrangement for converting an alternating current into a continuous current is called a commutator, from the Latin word *commutatus*, meaning "change."

In order to generate large quantities of electricity, more magnetism is necessary than can be supplied by permanent magnets and so coils of wire, which are really electromagnets but called "field coils," take their place. Permanent magnets are still used on the small dynamos called "hand generators" for telephone work, the magnetos for igniting gasoline engines and the small bicycle generators which light bicycle lamps.

It is quite easy to understand how an electric motor operates if the principle of the dynamo is carried in mind. A motor is really a

A TROLLEY–CAR MOTOR

The motor is entirely enclosed in an iron case to protect it from dirt, water and injury.

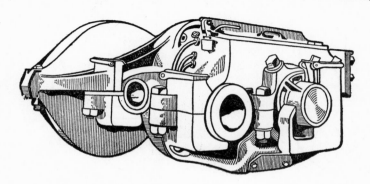

dynamo which is reversed, that is, instead of being driven by an engine or a turbine and generating an electric current it is fed with an electric current and used to drive machinery. In general construction there is but little difference between a dynamo and a motor, but there are differences in detail that make each machine better adapted to its own particular work.

Motors are built in a great variety of different sizes and shapes to suit some particular purpose. Some small motors called "universal"

INSIDE A SMALL UNIVERSAL MOTOR

These are the parts to be found inside the housing of the small universal electric motors used to drive sewing-machines, fans, hair dryers, mixers, vacuum cleaners, etc.

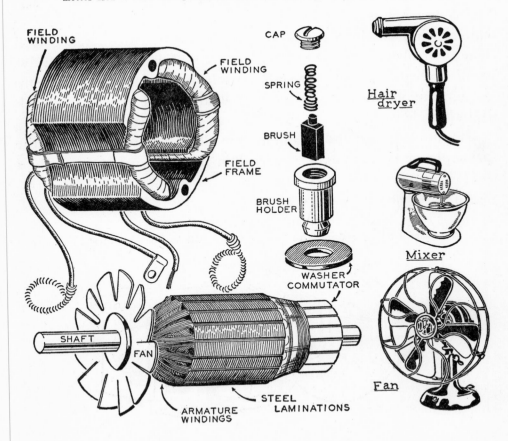

FIELD WINDING

CAP

FIELD WINDING

SPRING

Hair dryer

BRUSH

FIELD FRAME

BRUSH HOLDER

Mixer

WASHER
COMMUTATOR

SHAFT

FAN

Fan

ARMATURE WINDINGS

STEEL LAMINATIONS

motors will run on either alternating or direct current but the larger sizes are built especially for direct or alternating depending upon which is to be used and will not operate on both. It would be difficult to think of any means other than an electric motor which could be used with equal satisfaction to drive some machines. Motors may be "direct connected" to machinery without the use of elaborate systems of belts and shafting that is necessary when an engine is the source of power. For some purposes no other source of power can serve nearly so well as an electric motor.

UNIVERSAL MOTORS

The small motors of ⅟₂₀ to ⅙ horsepower which operate vacuum cleaners, small electric fans, cake mixers, sewing machines, electric drills, hair dryers and model railways are often of the universal type and consequently will operate on either direct current or 60-cycle alternating current. The field winding of these motors usually consists of two coils of wire covered with tape and supported in a field frame made of layers of steel known as laminations. The armature consists of a commutator and several coils of wire wound in narrow slots cut into a steel cylinder which is built of layers of steel pressed on a round steel shaft. The commutator consists of several copper bars formed into a cylinder but insulated from each other. The terminals of the armature coils are connected to the commutator bars. Current is led to the armature coils by means of two soft carbon brushes which press against the commutator. Some lightweight universal motors have a small fan pressed on the shaft inside the motor. The fan forces air through the motor and cools it.

INDUCTION MOTORS

Low-priced small electric fans, electric razors, record players, etc., are sometimes driven by a simple form of motor called an induction motor. The field windings and the field frame of this type of motor are similar to those used in a universal motor but the armature (called a rotor in this case) has no windings or commutator. The motor has no brushes. The power of this type of induction motor is low but they are used because they can be manufactured at smaller cost than other motors and because they do not get out of order easily.

SPLIT-PHASE MOTORS

Electric motors which render service in homes, workshops, farms and factories may be divided into two groups called "large" and "fractional horsepower" motors according to the power which they develop. Large motors are those which produce one horsepower or more. They are used principally in industry. Fractional-horsepower motors have many uses in the household and home workshop, where they drive such devices as washing machines, oil burners, coal stokers, saws, drill presses, lathes, air compressors and water pumps. The most common form of fractional-horsepower motor for these purposes is the split-phase motor. A split-phase consists of a stationary part, called the stator; a rotating part, called the rotor; and a centrifugal switch which is inside the motor. The rotor and stator are enclosed in a cast iron frame fitted with end plates which support the bearings for the shaft.

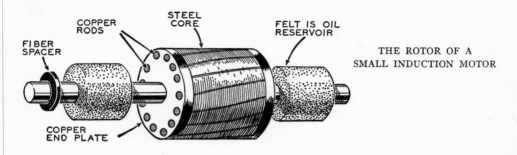

COPPER RODS

STEEL CORE

FELT IS OIL RESERVOIR

FIBER SPACER

COPPER END PLATE

THE ROTOR OF A
SMALL INDUCTION MOTOR

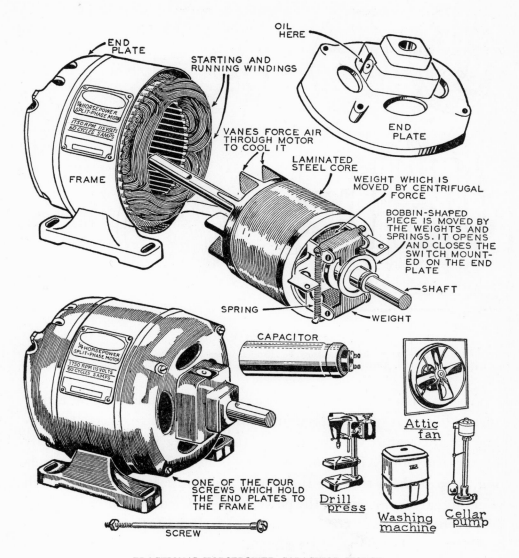

END PLATE

STARTING AND RUNNING WINDINGS

OIL HERE

END PLATE

¼ HORSEPOWER SPLIT-PHASE MOTOR
1750 R.P.M. 115 VOLTS
60 CYCLES 5 AMPS

FRAME

VANES FORCE AIR THROUGH MOTOR TO COOL IT

LAMINATED STEEL CORE

WEIGHT WHICH IS MOVED BY CENTRIFUGAL FORCE

BOBBIN-SHAPED PIECE IS MOVED BY THE WEIGHTS AND SPRINGS. IT OPENS AND CLOSES THE SWITCH MOUNTED ON THE END PLATE

SHAFT

SPRING

WEIGHT

¼ HORSEPOWER SPLIT-PHASE MOTOR
1750 R.P.M. 115 VOLTS
60 CYCLES 5 AMPS

CAPACITOR

Attic fan

ONE OF THE FOUR SCREWS WHICH HOLD THE END PLATES TO THE FRAME

SCREW

Drill press

Washing machine

Cellar pump

FRACTIONAL-HORSEPOWER CAPACITOR MOTOR

The sketch in the upper left-hand corner shows the motor with one end plate removed and the rotor pulled out so that the windings on the stator are exposed to view.

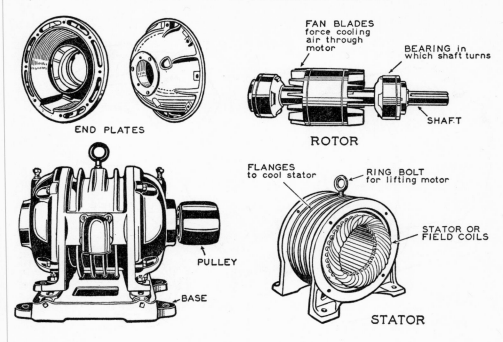

END PLATES

FAN BLADES
force cooling
air through
motor

BEARING in
which shaft turns

SHAFT

ROTOR

PULLEY

BASE

FLANGES
to cool stator

RING BOLT
for lifting motor

STATOR OR
FIELD COILS

STATOR

LARGE INDUSTRIAL MOTOR

The motors used to drive machinery in factories, mines, docks, etc., are called industrial
motors. They are ruggedly built to carry heavy loads for long periods.

A split-phase motor has no brushes or commutator. The armature is like that of an induction motor. There are two sets of windings on the stator. One winding is the starting winding, used only to start the motor. The other winding is a "main" or running winding, used both in starting the motor and while it is running. Both windings are connected to the power supply when the motor is started but as soon as the motor has reached nearly its full speed, the centrifugal switch automatically disconnects the starting winding.

In order to increase the power of a split-phase motor while it is starting and turning slowly, a capacitor is sometimes added to the stator circuit. The motor is then called a "capacitor motor." There are different kinds of capacitor motors. Some employ two capacitors.

CHAPTER ELEVEN

INDUCTION, ONE OF ELECTRICITY'S MOST USEFUL TRICKS

HAVE you ever been completely mystified by a card trick or a bit of sleight of hand and then when you were shown how the trick was done thought "how simple and easy that is"? And it was simple —after you knew how.

The same thing is true of electricity. Electricity does a lot of tricks which appear very simple when we can look back at them knowing all the things that we do in the twentieth century. But over one hundred years ago they were very mystifying, even to the men who discovered them.

One of electricity's most mysterious tricks is called *induction*— and it is also one of electricity's most obliging feats because it can be used for any number of purposes. The honor of discovering induction belongs to that grand old scientist, Michael Faraday. The experiments he made which disclosed how to build the first dynamo also revealed the knowledge which is used for making spark coils, transformers, alternating-current motors, certain types of electric furnaces and a good-sized list of other electrical equipment.

You will remember that Oersted discovered that a current of electricity flowing through a wire produces magnetism and that Faraday found out how to make magnetism produce a current of electricity. What then could be more logical than reversing the process and using the magnetic field produced by a current of electricity as the magnetic field for producing a current of electricity? So Fara-

173

day thought—and he was right—the trick works. When it is called by its full name, it is known as *electromagnetic induction.*

A POLYPHASE INDUCTION MOTOR

This may seem a complicated name to give a motor but it has a very definite meaning to an engineer. It is the type of motor most often used in large manufacturing plants.

You can easily find out what electromagnetic induction is by an experiment of your own. Wrap two or three layers of paper around a large nail and then wind about forty or fifty turns of insulated wire around one end of the nail. Wind a second similar coil of insulated wire around the other end of the nail. Connect one coil to a telephone receiver and the other to a battery. Listen to the telephone receiver. When the current from the battery is flowing through the one coil, you will not hear anything in the telephone receiver but if you make and break the circuit so as to shut the current on and off you will hear a clicking sound. The clicks are caused by an electric current *induced* in the coil connected to the telephone receiver by the *electromagnetism* created in the nail by the battery cur-

TELEPHONE INDUCTION COIL

The coil which Thomas A. Edison used in his telephone system makes use of the principle of induction and was a great improvement in the telephone art.

rent. When the battery current flows through the coil steadily, the magnetism in the nail is steady, but when you shut the current

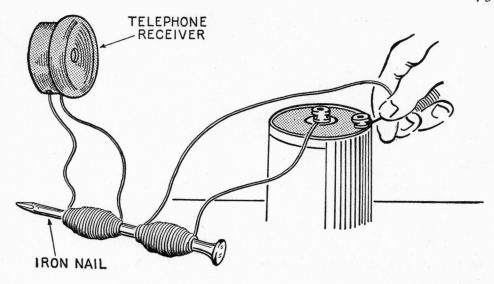

TELEPHONE RECEIVER

IRON NAIL

AN EXPERIMENT WITH ELECTROMAGNETIC INDUCTION

on and off the magnetic field changes. The current is induced in the second coil only when the magnetism is changing, that is, growing stronger or weaker.

It is said that after Michael Faraday discovered induction, someone asked him, "What is it good for?" "Good for?" said Faraday. "What good is a baby?" Just as one can never tell what a baby may grow up to be, neither could Faraday tell what induction might grow into.

One of the most useful of electrical devices is the transformer. In fact it might be called the whole backbone of the method used for distributing electric power over the vast network of wires which crisscross the country. The transformer grew out of Faraday's discovery. If two coils of wire are wound upon an iron ring, the arrangement makes a transformer. If an alternating current is sent through one of the coils, called the *primary*, an alternating current

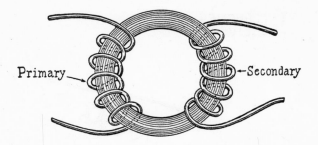

THE PRINCIPLE OF THE TRANSFORMER

A transformer consists of an iron ring supporting two coils of wire
called a primary and a secondary, as in the case of an induction coil.

will be created in the second or *secondary* coil. If the primary coil
has 100 turns and the secondary coil has 1,000 turns, the voltage of
the current induced in the secondary winding will be nearly ten
times as great as that in the primary. A transformer wound in this
manner transforms, or as it is called in electrical engineering "steps
up," the voltage of the current supplied to it. By reversing the arrangement and having ten turns on the secondary, and 100 on the
primary, it is possible to lower or step down the voltage of the
original current to one-tenth its former value. In all transformers
the voltages in the two coils are nearly proportional to the relative
number of turns of wire in the two coils.

Such a device is extremely useful in solving some of the problems
in electrical engineering. But it should be remembered that as in
other fields of science, so with electricity—it is impossible to get
something for nothing. Although a transformer raises or lowers the
voltage of an alternating current, the total power or number of watts
remains unaltered. If the voltage is increased, the amperage is correspondingly reduced and vice versa. The power of the current is not
changed except to be slightly decreased by certain inevitable losses
of energy that occur in the transformer itself.

The step-up transformer plays an important part in a power plant for raising the voltage of the current generated by the dynamos to a voltage suitable for sending it out over the long power lines. When high voltages are transmitted it is possible to use much smaller wires than with a lower voltage.

The voltage of the main power lines is too high to lead into a house. It would be dangerous. The current would leak, start fires and electrocute any one who touched the wires. So here is where the step-down transformer plays its part. It reduces the high transmission voltage of an alternating current to a voltage suitable for industrial and domestic uses. In large cities where the electric light and power wires run underground, the transformers are also placed underground in vaults or manholes. Where the lines run overhead

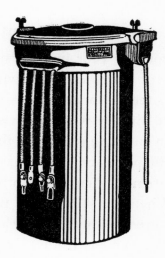

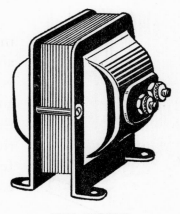

A LINE TRANSFORMER

A line or distribution transformer is used to reduce the high voltage of the power lines to 120 volts for use in homes or buildings. These transformers are sometimes placed underground in manholes. They are also mounted on electric-light poles.

BELL–RINGING TRANSFORMER

This little transformer reduces the 120-volt electric-light current to 6 or 8 volts so that it may be used to ring door bells. Although it is small enough to be held in the hand it operates in the same way as a large power transformer weighing several tons.

the transformers are usually placed on the poles. Sometimes the transformers necessary to supply large buildings or factories are too large to place on a pole and are installed in an underground vault or special room in the building.

Transformers are built in a great many shapes and sizes ranging from the smaller ones made for ringing bells, operating toy electric trains, neon signs, etc., to the huge affairs used in power houses.

The iron cores are always build up out of thin sheets of transformer steel. Magnetism cannot fluctuate or change rapidly enough in a solid iron core. That is why thin sheets or laminations, as they are called, are used.

HIGH–POTENTIAL
TRANSFORMER

This is one of the large oil-cooled transformers used to raise the voltage of the generators in a power station so that the energy can be sent over the lines without great loss.

HOW TO BUILD
AN INDUCTION COIL

If you put your fingers on the terminals of a dry cell you will not be able to feel a shock, unless a contact is made directly with a nerve through an open cut. The reason for this is that the skin possesses so much resistance that not enough current can flow to be felt. When the skin is wet, the resistance is greatly lowered and then sometimes the current from a dry cell can be felt with the fingers.

If wires connected to a dry cell are placed on the tip of the tongue, a current can flow because the tongue is wet. The amount of current is still very

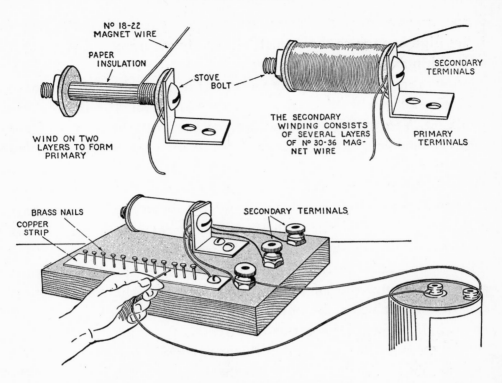

NO 18-22 MAGNET WIRE

PAPER INSULATION

STOVE BOLT

SECONDARY TERMINALS

WIND ON TWO LAYERS TO FORM PRIMARY

THE SECONDARY WINDING CONSISTS OF SEVERAL LAYERS OF NO 30-36 MAG-NET WIRE

PRIMARY TERMINALS

BRASS NAILS
COPPER STRIP

SECONDARY TERMINALS

AN EXPERIMENTAL INDUCTION COIL

An induction coil built from a small stove bolt and magnet wire will act as a transformer and raise the voltage of a dry cell sufficiently to give a slight shock.

small but it is enough to affect the sense of taste. The fact that the skin conducts electricity so much more easily when it is wet is the reason why it is dangerous to turn an electric light on or off when standing in a bathtub or while the hands and feet are wet. Sometimes an electric light socket is not properly insulated and although you may not be able to feel it with dry hands, the shock would be dangerous if your feet or hands were wet.

Farther back in this book, it was explained how voltage over-comes the resistance of an electric circuit and is necessary in order to force a current through. The voltage of a dry cell, about 1.5 volts, is not high enough so that it will ordinarily overcome the resistance of the skin and body.

However, you can raise the voltage of a single dry cell so that it will give a "shock" by means of an induction coil. It will not hurt you a bit. You will feel a prickling and tingling sensation which is entirely harmless. A few years ago toy shops used to sell small induction coils called "shocking coils" for boys to play with.

You can make your own shocking coil out of a one-quarter inch bolt and some wire. The bolt should be about two and one-half inches long. Fit the bolt with two washers cut out of heavy cardboard and soaked in shellac. Make the washers one inch in diameter. They should fit the bolt tightly. One washer should be placed against the inner side of the bolt head and the other on the inner side of the nut when the nut is screwed on the end of the bolt for about half an inch. Wrap two or three layers of paper around the bolt between the washers so that the primary winding which goes on next cannot come into contact with the core.

The primary winding consists of two layers of magnet wire wound over the paper-covered core. Any size of wire from No. 18 to 22 B. & S. gauge will do and it may be cotton, enamel or silk covered. Lead out the two terminal wires of the primary through suitable small holes punched through one of the cardboard washers.

Before starting to wind on the secondary, wrap two or three layers of paper over the primary. The secondary may be any size of magnet wire from No. 30 to 36 B. & S. gauge. Wind on enough wire to fill the space between the washers. As in the case of the primary, lead the terminals of the secondary coil out through holes in one of the cardboard washers and wrap the outside of the coil with two or three layers of paper to protect the fine wires underneath.

In order to operate the shocking coil, some sort of a current interrupter is necessary. This may be made out of a dozen brass nails driven into a block of wood. Perhaps the best way to set up the apparatus is to mount the coil on a little wooden base with a little brass or copper strap. Then the terminals of the primary and secondary winding can be led out to four binding posts. The current interrupter is arranged along one side of the base by driving the brass nails through a copper strip about four inches long and one-half inch wide. The copper connects all the nails together. One terminal of the primary leads to the strip. One terminal of a dry cell is connected to the other terminal of the primary winding. When the other battery wire is scraped along the nails, it makes and breaks the circuit. Every time the current flowing through the primary winding is "broken" a high voltage current is generated in the secondary by induction. If you connect two bare copper wires to the secondary, the person holding the wires will feel a distinct shock when the current interrupter is put in operation. A piece of metal connected to the end of each wire will make a better contact with the hands and increase the strength of the shock which is felt.

CHAPTER TWELVE

HOW ELECTRICAL POWER IS MADE AND DISTRIBUTED

THERE are very few things in this world that are not being constantly changed and improved. Almost every large factory has a laboratory of some sort and men whose duty it is to make improvements in the company's products and methods of manufacturing. This is especially true in the electrical and chemical industry. You often see or hear of new chemical products and the latest wonder of electricity, but you probably are unaware of the constant changes and improvements being made in generating and distributing electric power. The rates charged for electric power become steadily lower while the service improves. The electric lights seldom fail nowadays due to any fault at the generating station or in the power distribution system. A great transformation has taken place in the electrical power industry since it started. The old Edison station on Pearl Street in New York City which was the first power plant built for supplying electric current to the public would bear as much resemblance to a modern generating station as an hourglass does to a fine watch.

Some of the large power companies allow groups of school children in charge of their teachers to visit the stations. A "pass" must be secured beforehand. Whenever there is an opportunity to see one of these intresting places it will be well worthwhile to go.

The most striking feature about the generating room of a large power station is its silence. The giant dynamos, revolving at a rate perhaps of 3,000 times a minute, are very quiet. Only a pleasant hum is to be heard. The engines or turbines too run very quietly, although here may be enough power to generate electricity for all the factories and homes of a whole countryside.

All large public power-stations generate alternating current with the exception of a small amount of direct current produced to use in the plant itself for operating some of the control equipment and supplying field current to the dynamos.

The speed of the machines is very carefully controlled. Sometimes several generators or even several power stations feed into the same lines and consequently the alternations from these different sources must be kept in exact step with each other. This is done so accurately that it might almost be said that the frequency never varies a "hair's breadth."

The reason that alternating current is generated for electric lights and power is because it is much more economical to send out the current at a high voltage and then reduce it to a low voltage again at the place where it is needed. The voltage of a direct current cannot be changed up or down easily. If currents of low voltage

POWER TRANSMISSION

The current generated at a low station passes through transformers which induce currents of high tension or voltage in the transmission line.

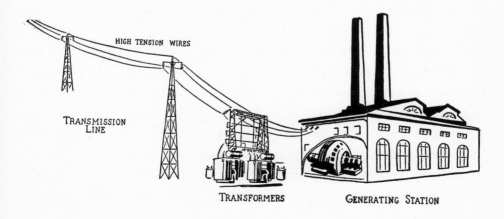

HIGH TENSION WIRES

TRANSMISSION LINE

TRANSFORMERS   GENERATING STATION

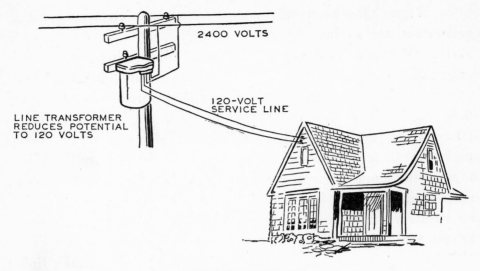

2400 VOLTS

120-VOLT
SERVICE LINE

LINE TRANSFORMER
REDUCES POTENTIAL
TO 120 VOLTS

POWER DISTRIBUTION

The high-tension current of the transmission lines is reduced at transformer stations to approximately 2,400 volts and sent out over underground or overhead feeders. Line transformers again reduce the voltage to 120–240 volts before the current enters a house.

(120 to 240 volts) were sent out over the power mains the wires in some localities would have to be as big around as a telegraph pole. Another difficulty that is avoided by using alternating current and its accompanying transformers is that with almost any other system the customers nearest to the power house would receive current at a higher voltage than those farther away.

The current which is to be delivered a long distance is sent out at a very high voltage over wires suspended from insulators on steel towers. You have probably seen these "transmission lines," as they are called. This high tension (high voltage) current is sent through transformer stations at various points and sub-stations from which it is distributed to the immediate neighborhood. The power which is consumed near a generating station usually goes out over underground cables or cables carried on poles.

A large, steam-driven generating station consumes vast quantities of coal and requires a plentiful supply of water. For that reason you will find that an electrical power plant is usually built on the banks of a river where there is an ample supply of water and coal can be brought in on barges cheaply and easily. When the coal arrives it is unloaded by machinery and stored in huge piles from which it is carried to the "hoppers." It is then taken by some sort of a mechanical conveyor to the small hoppers close to the furnace into which it is fed by mechanical stokers. The steam from the giant boilers is collected in large pipes and led to the generating room where it passes into the engines or

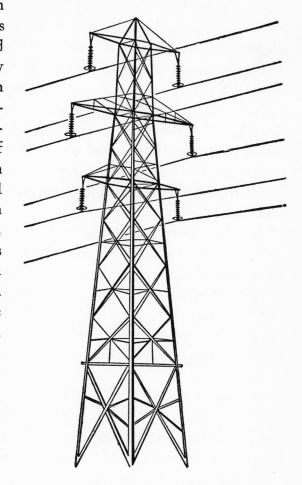

A TRANSMISSION TOWER

Transmission towers are made of steel. The wires are supported from long corrugated insulators. Transmission line voltages of 150,000 volts or more are not unusual.

turbines. Having done its work, the steam passes to a condenser where it is cooled and condensed back to water. It is then freed from oil and grease and sent back to the boilers to be reconverted into steam. Most of the water used in the station is required to keep the condensers cool and this is usually taken from a river or canal. Every possible economy is exercised everywhere in a modern generating station. The tendency now is to have fewer and larger stations.

The 120-volt domestic electric lighting system and the devices for which it supplies the power, such as lamps, stoves, motors, irons, toasters, clocks, etc., should never be tampered with by the young electrical experimenter or any inexperienced person. The average boy or man who has not had practical experience in electrical work seldom has the knowledge to repair or adjust anything but the most minor troubles with such equipment without the risk of getting into trouble.

All changes or major repairs in the wiring of a house or building should be the work of a first-class electrician. The Board of Fire Insurance Underwriters has made certain rules with which such work must comply if the insurance on a house or building is to remain in effect. In case of a fire which was due to an electrical fault, it might be impossible to collect the insurance if it is shown that there was any unapproved wiring in the building.

FUSES

One of the first and most important parts of any electrical system is the fuse. The way in which fuses function and the purpose they serve has already been explained. Any properly installed wiring or electrical device protected with the necessary fuse is never a fire hazard and need never be a source of worry.

When a fuse blows out it is due to a good reason.

The fuse is too small, there is a short circuit in the line or an "overload" caused by operating too many lamps, motors, flatirons or other devices at the same time. If you find out what was connected to the line at the time and how much current each device should draw, you will know whether or not the total amount was enough to blow out the fuse or a short circuit was the cause of the trouble.

If the fuse "blew" due to an overload, put in a larger fuse, *if the line will stand it*. An electrician can tell you how many amperes the line will carry.

If only part of the lights in the house fail to operate and a fuse has blown out, you will find that it is a "branch" fuse which needs to be replaced. If all the lights go out and the trouble is due to a blown-out fuse, it is a "main" fuse which has burned.

Before you attempt to touch any fuses, *turn the main switch off*. Use a flashlight to see what you are doing. Try to find out what caused the "blow-out" before putting in a new fuse. It is best to disconnect any electrical appliances such as fans and flatirons, and leave only the lights in the circuit.

Replace the burned out fuse or fuses with new ones and turn on the main switch. If the lights burn and the fuses do not blow out again immediately, you have removed the source of trouble but should ascertain what it was, an overload or a short circuit caused by a defective cord or plug, etc. If the fuse blows out again and you cannot locate the trouble, there is just one thing to do—send for an electrician.

Fuses are rated and marked to indicate the number of amperes which they will carry safely without burning out. The figures 10, 15, 30 or whatever it may be are stamped on the bottom. If you calculate the amount of current required on a circuit you can easily figure the right size of fuse to give proper protection and protect the line. Use the size next larger than the number of amperes actually required. Suppose that the lamps or other devices on the circuit would consume about 1,000 watts if all were in operation at the same time. This would mean a current of about 10 amperes at 120 volts. There is a 10 ampere size of fuse but it would be too small. Use a 15 ampere fuse instead.

Almost all incandescent lamps are marked to indicate the number of watts they consume. So are electric flatirons, toasters, small motors, etc. A knowledge of the amount of energy used by the lamps and electrical appliances in your home will prevent overloading any of the circuits or burning out the fuses.

Remember that electric motors draw more current for a few seconds when they are starting and picking up speed than they do when they are running. A motor which is overloaded or called upon to do more work than it should will draw more current than it would under a normal load.

Probably the most common reason why lamps, flatirons, and other electrical appliances cause a fuse to blow out is a fault in the flexible wire or "cord" used to connect them to the current outlet. Putting

High Voltages

are  Dangerous

ELECTRICITY IS WORTHY OF RESPECT

The human body offers considerable resistance to an electric current but when the voltage is high enough to overcome that resistance serious burns or even death may result. Linemen and electrical workers avoid live or "hot" wires as they call lines carrying dangerous currents. They wear rubber gloves and special shoes as an aid in avoiding accidents.

the plug in and out of the outlet and straining upon the connecting wires often wears the insulation on the wires where they pass through the plug—or the connection becomes broken at the plug. Look over this part of all equipment occasionally to see that it is in good order.

The ordinary electric light socket was not designed to carry the 500 watts or more of electrical energy required by flatirons and toasters. If you shut off the current by turning the switch in the socket when one of these appliances is connected, it will "arc" and burn the little metal contacts inside. It will not be long before the socket will burn out. Shut the current off by pulling out the plug instead of turning the switch.

Washing machines, vacuum cleaners, sewing machines, phonographs, and other devices provided with an electric motor should be kept properly oiled and lubricated so that the motor is perfectly free to start. Too much oil is just as wrong as too little, because it becomes thick and gummy and causes friction. It also gets on the commutator. When the bearings get gummy with thick oil, clean them with kerosene.

Here are two very good DON'TS for anyone who proposes to repair any troubles with the 120-volt electric lighting circuit:

Don't attempt to make any connections or look for trouble without first shutting the current off the line.

Don't touch any tools or your fingers to any wires or metal parts of a circuit while you are standing on a cement or dirt floor or while you are in contact with a sink, bathtub, or radiator.

AUTOMATIC CIRCUIT-BREAKERS

Power plants and factories use circuit-breakers to protect their wiring and equipment from the damage which would be caused by an overload or by a short circuit. Circuit-breakers serve the same purpose as fuses; they shut off the current when trouble occurs. When a fuse acts to protect a circuit, the fuse "burns out" and must be replaced by a new one. Circuit-breakers cost more than fuses but do not have to be replaced. When a circuit-breaker acts, the breaker mechanism moves and opens a switch. Nothing burns out and nothing has to be renewed in a circuit-breaker. When the trouble which caused the circuit-breaker to act has been located and removed, it is necessary only to move the handle of the circuit-breaker back to the "on" position. In Chapter Seven, there is an illustration of an automatic circuit-breaker.

Many modern homes are equipped with circuit-breakers instead of fuses. An automatic circuit-breaker eliminates the necessity for fuses. The mechanism of the circuit-breakers used in residences is enclosed in a steel cabinet, usually located in a hallway or kitchen.

CHAPTER THIRTEEN

THE ELECTRICAL SYSTEM OF AN AUTOMOBILE

THERE are several million automobiles in daily use in the U. S. A. and all but very few of them use the internal combustion engine as their motive power. During the first two decades of this century three forms of motive power were used to drive automobiles. Most cars to be seen on the roads during that period were propelled by internal combustion engines like the gasoline engine used in today's automobiles. There were a few whose motive power was supplied by a steam engine and boiler. In the large cities, many trucks and some passenger cars were driven by electric motors. Large storage batteries carried by these vehicles furnished electric current for their motors.

Steam-propelled automobiles have disappeared; they are to be found only in museums.

There are still a few electric trucks on the roads and many electric loading trucks are in use in railway yards and factories, but the internal combustion engine is now supreme as a motive power for vehicles.

Gasoline and oil are the fuels whose energy propels the modern automobile but electricity is an almost indispensable assistant in its operation. The modern automobile without its electrical equipment would not be nearly so flexible and practicable for the average person to drive.

The ignition system is not the only electrical equipment on an automobile. An electric motor starts or cranks the engine. The electric starter made it possible for almost everyone to drive an automobile. Fewer people would own cars if they had to start the engine with a hand crank. It is both difficult and dangerous.

A generator recharges the battery which drives the starting motor and furnishes current for the ignition, horn, and lights.

The electrical system of an automobile is usually what is called the single wire type. The various "units" such as the generator, starting motor, storage battery, horn, electric lights, etc., are all "grounded" on the frame and engine. In other words, the return connection is made through the various metal parts of the chassis.

A heavy cable leads from the starter motor to the starter switch and then from the switch to one terminal of the battery. The other terminal of the battery is grounded, that is, connected to the engine. So is one terminal of the starting motor. Pressing the starter switch completes the circuit and cranks the motor.

The battery is a common part of the ignition, lighting, and horn circuits. Since one terminal of the horn, lights, and ignition system is grounded, a wire from the other terminal of each to the ungrounded terminal of the battery is all that is necessary to complete the circuit in each case.

THE IGNITION SYSTEM OF AN AUTOMOBILE

In order to understand the ignition system of an automobile, you should first know what an induction coil is, in case you do not already know.

Usually under the hood or on the dash of almost every automobile there is a little cylindrical case which contains two coils of wire wound around an iron core. One coil consists of about 100 turns of comparatively coarse wire while the other contains from 9,000 to 25,000 turns of fine hair-like wire. This little device is called an *induction* coil. The common name for it is a "spark" coil.

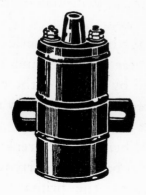 

AN AUTOMOBILE IGNITION COIL AND CUTOUT

An ignition coil (sometimes called a spark coil) is an induction coil which raises the 6-volt current of the storage battery to several thousand volts so that it will jump across the spark plugs and ignite the mixture of gasoline and air in the cylinders. The little device called an automatic cutout disconnects the storage battery from the generator when an automobile engine slows down or stops and thus prevents the battery current from being wasted (by flowing back through the generator).

It is a simple arrangement for increasing the voltage of a battery current to such a high potential that it will jump across the plugs and explode the charge in the engine cylinder. It will raise a six volt current to 10,000 volts or more. A German-French mechanician named Heinrich Ruhmkorff was the inventor of the device used as a "spark coil," but a man named Lenoir was the first to use it for ignition or "firing" an engine. He did this nearly one hundred years ago. Many millions of coils have been made for engines since that day.

The core of a spark coil is a bundle of iron wires. A solid iron core cannot be used because the core must be capable of being quickly magnetized and demagnetized. For that reason iron wires are better than a solid bar. The coil of coarse wire wrapped around the core is called the "primary" winding. The outside winding, wound around both the core and the primary, is the "secondary."

The primary and the secondary are carefully insulated from each other.

The primary is connected to the storage battery, in series with an interrupter or "breaker." The interrupter "makes" and "breaks" the circuit. It is a little switch, operated by a cam on the engine so as to turn the current on and off repeatedly. It is carefully adjusted so that the current will be cut off just at the right time.

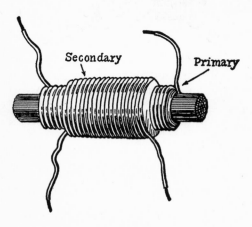

INDUCTION COIL

One of the greatest contributions ever made to electrical science was Michael Faraday's discovery of induction. An induction coil consists of two coils of wire, a primary and a secondary, wound around an iron core.

Whenever the breaker closes, the battery current flows through the primary winding and magnetizes the core. Then when the switch opens, the magnetism suddenly disappears and a current of very high voltage is induced in the secondary. This high-voltage current will jump through the air nearly one-half an inch.

A six cylinder engine fires or explodes three times for each revolution. The breaker switch is connected to the engine so that it opens and closes three times each revolution at just the right instant to fire the proper cylinder. The high-voltage current from the secondary of the coil is directed to the proper spark plug by a revolving switch called the distributor.

THE HIGH-TENSION MAGNETO

Many foreign—built cars and also some of the motor-trucks made in this country are equipped with high-tension magnetos in place

HIGH–TENSION MAGNETO

A magneto is an electric generator which uses permanent magnets for its field. The high-tension magneto is a combination of an alternating-current generator and an induction coil. It is used to supply high-voltage current for the ignition system of a gasoline engine.

of a spark coil for igniting the engine. A high-tension magneto is really an alternating-current generator with a sort of induction coil built into the armature—or it might be described in just the contrary way by saying that a high-tension magneto is a spark coil which generates its own current.

The armature winding serves two purposes. It is the winding in which the alternating current produced by the magneto is generated and it is also the primary of an induction coil. The current flowing through the armature is interrupted by a "breaker switch" mounted on the magneto shaft and operating just like the one used with battery and coil ignition. Breaking the current in the primary produces a very high voltage in the secondary and this is led to the proper spark plug by a distributor switch. Only two sparks can be obtained from a magneto for each revolution and so the magneto is geared to the engine to produce a spark for each cylinder in its turn. A magneto has no field coils. The field magnetism is supplied by permanent magnets.

THE STARTING MOTOR

In order to start a steam engine or an electric motor it is only necessary to turn on the steam or the electric current, as the case may be. But with a gasoline engine it is a different story. The engine must be "turned over" so as to draw a fresh mixture of air

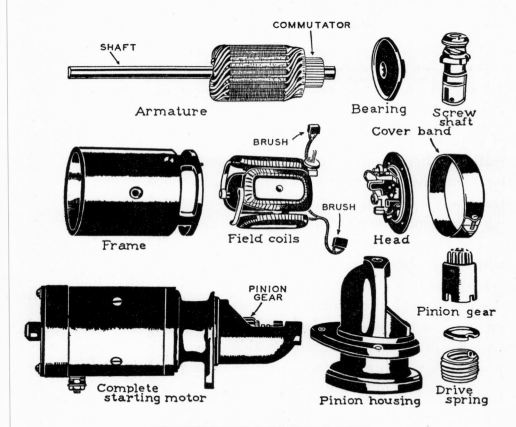

STARTING MOTOR WITH BENDIX DRIVE

An automobile starting motor is a very compact and powerful unit which puts forth a tremendous effort all out of proportion to its size. The average starting motor will develop more than one horsepower for a few seconds. The illustration shows a typical starting motor and also the parts of which it is made.

and gasoline into one of the cylinders. The first automobiles were started with cranks, turned by hand. It was a risky job. A person had to be strong and on the alert to make sure that the engine did not "kick" and throw the crank back with great force. Many people were badly hurt while attempting to start their cars with a crank. Various sorts of spring and compressed-air starters were developed but none of them was quite satisfactory. The best method proved to be an electric motor driven with current furnished by a storage battery. It is the method still used.

The starter is a specially built series-wound electric motor designed to develop a great deal of power for a short time when supplied with current from a six- or twelve-volt storage battery. The oil in a cold engine is thick and gummy and it requires more power to crank the engine when it is cold than when it is warm. Starting a cold engine will require as much as 300 amperes of current but when it is warm it usually requires only 100 amperes. Such heavy currents make it necessary to build starting motors with field coils of copper ribbon and with armatures wound with copper bars instead of wire.

The starting motor is usually geared so that it turns over twelve to fifteen times for each revolution of the engine. Gearing the motor to the engine is accomplished with a clever little device called an "inertia pinion." The "Bendix drive" which you may have heard of in reference to an automobile is an inertia pinion. This arrangement makes it possible for the motor to be geared to the engine only during the cranking operation. The inertia pinion is automatically moved lengthwise on the motor shaft as the motor reaches speed, thus becoming engaged with the gear mounted on the engine flywheel. As soon as the engine begins to operate under its own power at a speed in excess of that at which it was driven by the starting motor, the inertia pinion is automatically disengaged.

THE STORAGE BATTERY

Electrical engineers often use the words "primary battery" in referring to a battery made up of the type of cells that Volta invented, that is, a cell in which a metal slowly dissolves in a chemical solution and liberates electricity. A primary battery to furnish current for an automobile starting motor would not be practical. It would have to be too large; it would be too expensive and unsuitable in many ways.

There is also another sort of battery which is called a secondary battery and it is suitable for use in an automobile. A secondary battery is commonly spoken of in the United States as a storage battery. In Great Britain it is called an accumulator. Before a storage battery can produce a current of electricity, a direct current must be sent through it from another battery or from a generator.

There are millions of storage batteries in daily use in automobiles for starting, ignition and lighting. Storage batteries are also used for other purposes. For example, they are used to propel submarines. Every central telephone office is equipped with large storage batteries as a "standby" source of power in the event the power which drives the generators supplying current to the telephone system should fail.

Each cell of a storage battery delivers approximately two volts. Three or six cells connected in series so as to deliver six or twelve volts are almost universally employed in automobiles. Each cell of an automobile storage battery consists of several lead plates immersed in a dilute solution of sulfuric acid. Separators made of wood, hard rubber or glass wool and inserted between the plates prevent the plates from touching each other. The plates are cast from lead in the form of a grid and are filled with a lead "paste." The paste in the positive plates is lead peroxide; that in the negative plates is spongy lead. There are usually from 13 to 19 plates in each cell. The capacity of a storage cell is measured in "ampere hours." An ampere hour is the amount of current represented by one ampere flowing for one hour. A 100-ampere-hour cell will deliver

2 amperes for 50 hours
5 amperes for 20 hours
10 amperes for 10 hours

A SIX–VOLT AUTOMOBILE STORAGE BATTERY

This is the familiar battery for supplying current to the ignition system, electric lights, and starting motor of an automobile.

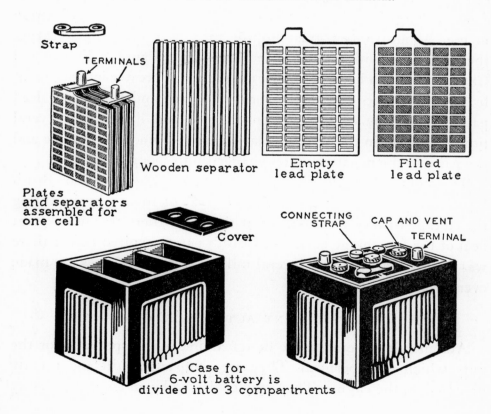

The principle upon which the cell operated was discovered by a Frenchman named Gantherot at about the time Michael Faraday first went to work at the Royal Institution. However, it was not until fifty years later that the principle was put to practical use and the first storage cell was built. It was called a Planté cell after the man who made it. Planté's cells consisted of two thin sheets of lead immersed in dilute sulfuric acid. The cells would apparently store up an electric current which was passed through them. They did not actually store electricity but the result was the same. Current passed through a Planté cell, to "charge" it, really brought about chemical changes in the lead plates which caused them to produce a current of electricity of their own.

For a long time, Planté's invention was the only storage battery in use. About 1880 a great improvement was made by smearing the lead plates with a paste of red lead. Then Faure in France and Charles F. Brush here in America made a still greater improvement by devising plates cast in the form of a grid and filled with lead paste. When the cells had been charged and discharged several times the paste in the positive plates changed into lead dioxide and the paste in the negative plates changed into spongy lead.

The storage batteries in use today are Brush's invention. Brush lost the opportunity to make a great deal of money by inventing the storage battery too soon, for at that time there was not a great deal of use for storage batteries. Brush's patent expired before there was a large market. Now several million storage batteries are made every year for automobiles.

THE DIRECT-CURRENT AUTOMOBILE GENERATOR

Automobile generators are designed and built especially for the duty which they perform. They are compactly built and usually mounted on the engine. They may be driven by an engine accessory

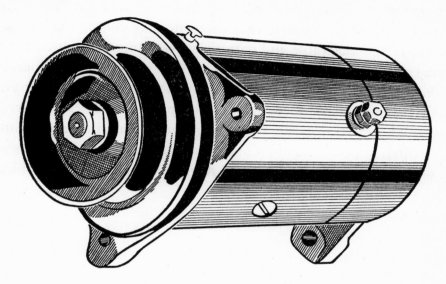

AN AUTOMOBILE GENERATOR

This generator is equipped with a pulley so that it can be driven with a V belt. A fan is built into the rear face of the pulley so that air is drawn through the motor to cool it.

drive shaft or by a belt from a pulley on an extension of the engine camshaft or the crankshaft.

An automobile generator is usually cylindrical in shape. Inside the cylindrical cast iron frame are two field windings, an armature and the brushes. Some generators have two brushes and some have three.

Every automobile has a meter or an indicator which shows whether or not the battery is being charged. This meter is mounted on the instrument panel through which passes all the current going either in or out of the battery and generator. Some meters show the number of amperes which are flowing and whether they are flowing in or out of the battery. Others indicate whether or not the battery is low or fully charged.

There are periods when an automobile engine is not running or when it is running so slowly that the generator does not charge the battery. If the generator and battery were connected at such times, current from the battery would flow back through the generator and be wasted. To prevent this, all automobile generators are provided with an automatic switch which opens and closes the circuit between the generator and the storage battery at the proper time. This switch is called a cutout and it is usually enclosed in the steel box which contains the current and voltage regulators. It resembles a

THE PARTS OF AN AUTOMOBILE GENERATOR

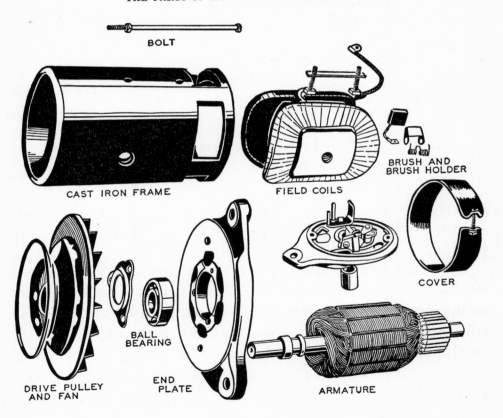

BOLT

CAST IRON FRAME

FIELD COILS

BRUSH AND BRUSH HOLDER

COVER

DRIVE PULLEY AND FAN

BALL BEARING

END PLATE

ARMATURE

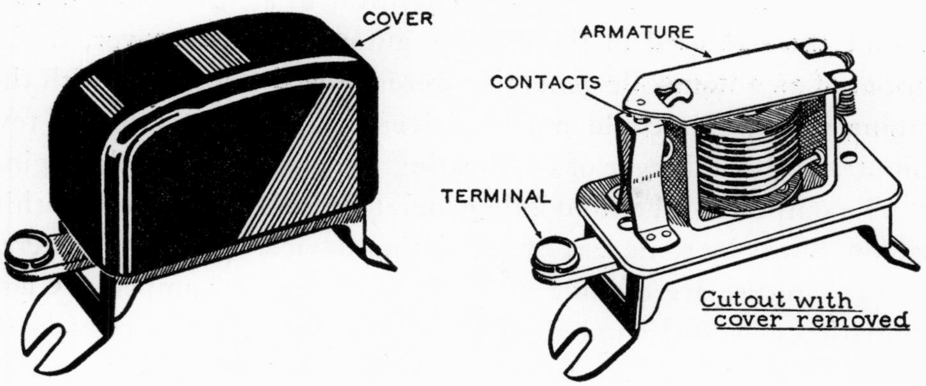

COVER

ARMATURE

CONTACTS

TERMINAL

Cutout with
cover removed

THE CUTOUT

This device automatically disconnects the battery from the generator when the engine is not running or is running too slowly to charge the battery. It automatically connects the battery again when the generator is turning at sufficient speed to charge the battery.

relay in appearance. The contacts on the cutout are normally held apart by a spring. The spring is so adjusted that as soon as the generator turns fast enough to produce 6½ to 7 volts (on a 6-volt system), the pull of the electromagnet in the cutout becomes strong enough to overcome the pull of the spring and so bring the contacts together. When the contacts touch each other, the battery is connected to the generator. When the engine stops or slows down so that the voltage of the generator falls below that of the battery, the spring overcomes the pull of the electromagnet so that the contacts separate and open the circuit.

REGULATORS FOR AUTOMOBILE GENERATORS

The voltage and current output of a generator increase in direct proportion to the generator's speed. In other words, the faster a car is driven, the faster its generator turns and the greater is the output of volts and amperes. If continued too long, a heavy charging current from the generator would be harmful to a fully charged battery of the size used in the average automobile. Moreover, if the output of an automobile generator were allowed to increase with the engine speed, cars could not be driven fast for more than a few minutes without danger of overheating the generator and damaging it. The output of all automobile generators is therefore held within narrow limits by some sort of regulating device. The large generators now in use are capable of producing 25 to 35 amperes. Close regulation of voltage and amperage is therefore more necessary today than ever before. Vibrating relays are used to regulate both current and voltage in many recently manufactured cars. When an automobile equipped with these regulators is driven fast, the relays go into action and prevent too much current from flowing into the battery. They do this by cutting a resistance intermittently in and

CURRENT AND VOLTAGE REGULATORS FOR GENERATOR

The unit shown at the left consists of a cutout and a voltage regulator. The right-hand unit includes a cutout, current regulator and voltage regulator. The units are shown without the metal cover which protects them from dirt and injury.

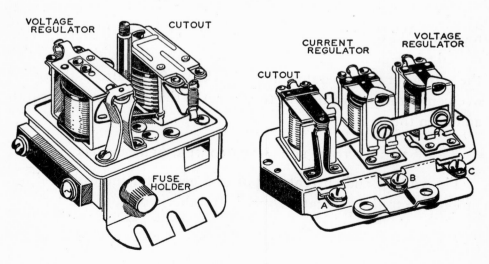

out of the field winding circuit in the generator. The regulators, together with the automatic cutout, are enclosed in a steel box mounted on top of the generator. Sometimes only a cutout and a voltage regulator are provided but many cars are equipped with a cutout, a voltage regulator and a current regulator.

THE ALTERNATING-CURRENT AUTOMOBILE GENERATOR (ALTERNATOR)

The electrical current requirements of automobiles have been increasing quite rapidly (doubling every ten years) and have reached the point where the conventional direct-current generator is not quite adequate. The size and design of the generator could be changed so as to obtain a little more output but this would add to the weight and cost of the generator out of proportion to the gain in output.

The problem has been solved by replacing the DC generator with a simple, compact, lightweight, reasonable-in-cost *alternator*.

The automobile alternator generates current at low speeds. The conventional DC generator does not usually produce any current at all when the engine is idling.

The prime purpose of the storage battery in an automobile is to start the engine. The purpose of the generator is to replace the charge taken from the battery to start the car and to supply the current for operating the headlights, taillights, radio, defroster, heater, power seats and windows and a variety of other electrical conveniences. The amount of current produced by a direct-current generator varies with the engine speed. A car has to be going more than 25 miles per hour for the conventional generator to develop its full current output. At engine idling speeds and in slow traffic there is generally no generator output and the battery must supply current for ignition, lights, etc. The battery is slowly discharged at low engine speeds and unless the car is soon driven fast enough and long enough to recharge the

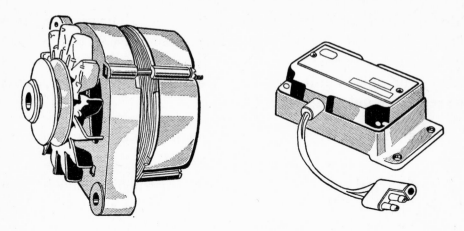

THE MOTOROLA AUTOMOBILE ALTERNATOR AND
TRANSISTORIZED VOLTAGE REGULATOR

battery, the battery may be trying to meet the demand for current while in a half-charged condition. This increases gasoline consumption, shortens battery life and makes starting more difficult, especially during cold weather.

An automobile alternator will *charge the battery* when the engine is *idling* and while the car is driven slowly in city traffic. An alternator is so superior to the conventional direct-current generator that eventually all cars will be equipped with them at the factory. Chrysler Corporation was the first manufacturer to offer the alternator as standard equipment.

A Motorola alternator is shown in one of the illustrations. It is about one-half the size of the common direct-current generator. An AC generator and a DC generator operate on the same principle but in the Motorola alternator the moving parts are reversed. In a DC generator a conductor wound around an armature rotates in a magnetic field. In the AC generator or alternator the conductor is stationary and the magnetic field rotates.

A rectifier consisting of six silicon diodes is connected to the alternator to rectify the AC current and change it to DC. These diodes permit current to flow from the alternator to the battery and to any other electrical devices but will not allow current to pass from the battery to the alternator. Consequently no cutout relay is required. A voltage regulator is the only control required with an alternator.

The Motorola voltage regulator is a transistorized device using no mechanical contacts or relays. There are no parts in the regulator to wear or get out of order. It consists of two transistors, one zener diode, seven resistors and one thermistor. A thermistor is a temperature-controlled solid state device. A storage battery requires more voltage in order to remain satisfactorily charged in cold weather and less voltage in warm weather. The thermistor automatically increases the charging voltage in cold weather and decreases it in warm weather. This is a feature which is entirely lacking in the mechanical or relay type voltage controls.

TRANSISTOR IGNITION

The weakest part of an automobile engine is usually the ignition system unless it is a modern transistor-controlled system. Since about 1910 automobiles have employed a mechanical engine-driven switch called a breaker to "make and break" the current in the primary of a spark coil and produce a high-voltage spark at the plugs. The current supplied the spark coil is interrupted by the breaker contacts (called points) about 12,000 times for every mile a 6-cylinder car is driven. The breaker is actually an overloaded device. It is pushed to its limit in trying to meet the spark needs of modern high-compression engines. Because the breaker points are closed for such a short time for each spark at high engine speed, the spark plugs do not receive a spark which is as hot and strong as desirable. When a conventional ignition system is used, the current of 2 to 10 amperes

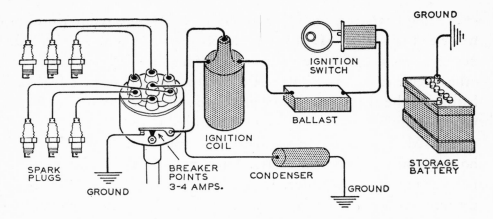

SPARK PLUGS · GROUND · BREAKER POINTS 3-4 AMPS. · IGNITION COIL · CONDENSER · IGNITION SWITCH · BALLAST · GROUND · STORAGE BATTERY · GROUND

CONVENTIONAL IGNITION SYSTEM FOR A 6–CYLINDER AUTOMOBILE

The breaker points open three times for each revolution of the engine, and each time interrupt the current flowing through the primary of the ignition coil. Each time the primary current is interrupted a high-voltage current is induced in the secondary of the ignition coil and produces a spark at one of the plugs. The breaker points eventually become pitted and worn by the current.

TRANSISTORIZED IGNITION SYSTEM

In this system a transistor interrupts the current flowing through the primary of the ignition coil. The breaker points merely "trigger" the ignition. The breaker points carry such a small amount of current in this system, they do not become pitted and worn.

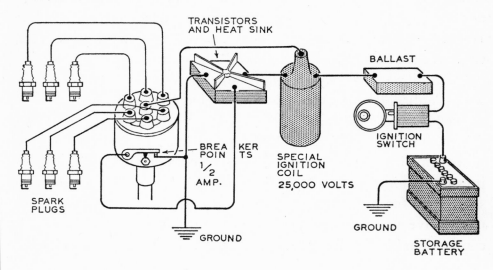

TRANSISTORS AND HEAT SINK · BALLAST · SPARK PLUGS · BREAKER POINTS 1/2 AMP. · SPECIAL IGNITION COIL 25,000 VOLTS · IGNITION SWITCH · GROUND · GROUND · STORAGE BATTERY

which flows through the points, especially at low speeds, overheats the points. The heat oxidizes and pits the points. Then the car does not start easily or run smoothly until the points have been replaced. If an engine is to be kept 100 per cent "tuned," the breaker points should be inspected or replaced (if necessary) every 2,000 to 5,000 miles.

Transistor ignition systems eliminate breaker problems. A transistor ignition system will deliver fat, high voltage sparks to the plugs, even at top engine speeds. Longer breaker point life and easier starting are other advantages. Transistor ignition makes it possible to idle along at five miles per hour in high gear.

There are three systems of transistor ignition now in use. The simplest is that supplied by Ford and used in most owner installed systems. A transistor replaces the breaker points. It is an electronic switch with no moving points to oxidize or pit. If kept cool it can handle safely several times as much current as breaker points. The breaker points are still used in a transistor ignition system but only to "trigger" the transistor. Only about ⅓ ampere passes through the breaker points and consequently they will remain in good condition for at least 50,000 miles. It is probable that more and more cars will be equipped with transistor ignition systems until the latter become standard equipment on all automobiles.

CHAPTER FOURTEEN

SENDING MESSAGES THROUGH SPACE

THE idea of sending messages through space without wires is not as new as is generally supposed, for attempts at signalling in this way were made in the sixteenth century with a kind of magnetic wireless telegraph. Nothing came of these first efforts, and until comparatively few years ago when ships left port nothing was heard from them until they reached their destination. There was no way of communicating between the shore and a vessel far out to sea. Then the wireless telegraph was invented and all was changed. Messages could be sent through space for hundreds of miles. Now all vessels of any size carry radio. (The term radio has replaced the old term wireless.) The law requires all passenger vessels to carry such equipment. Many of the largest ocean liners are provided with radio telephone equipment which makes it possible for passengers aboard one of these vessels in the middle of the Atlantic ocean to be connected with any telephone belonging to the Bell system.

THE WIRELESS TELEGRAPH

The first means of communicating between the land and ships at sea was by means of the dot and dash signals of the wireless telegraph. This was the predecessor of that which we call radio. The old apparatus seems crude when contrasted with modern equipment. It was bulky, noisy, and inefficient in comparison. A large induction coil or transformer which would deliver 20,000 to 50,000 volts, a battery of large Leyden jars, a telegraph key, a coil of wire or metal ribbon called an inductance and a spark gap for discharging the Leyden jars were used for sending the messages. The apparatus was connected to an antenna or system of aerial wires, and when the key was pressed generated electromagnetic or Hertzian waves which are a sort of invisible light. The waves travelled out through space and when they struck another antenna or aerial, generated feeble alternating currents corresponding to the dots and dashes made by pressing the key at the transmitting station. When the tiny alternating currents in the receiving antenna were passed through a device called a detector they made sounds in a telephone receiver and the message could be read. There were all sorts of detector devices in use—crystal, electrolytic, magnetic, and audion.

THE INVISIBLE ELECTROMAGNETIC WAVES
WHICH HERTZ DISCOVERED

The electromagnetic waves which made wireless telegraphy and radio possible were discovered by a professor of physics at Karlsruhe, Germany. Heinrich Hertz was his name. That is why they are sometimes called Hertzian waves. Three other scientists, Sir Oliver Lodge, E. Branly, and Professor Popoff, discovered how to use Hertzian waves for sending signals through space. They invented the first wireless telegraph systems.[1] Then a young man named Guglielmo Marconi started experimenting with the apparatus which Branly, Popoff, and Lodge had invented and found that he could greatly improve it. He succeeded in making it more sensitive and efficient. When Marconi was twenty-two years old he went to England and started experimenting with wireless for the British Post

---

[1] In 1883 Professor A. E. Dolbear actually succeeded in sending signals through space without wires. Dolbear took out a patent for his system and in 1884 gave a demonstration at the Electrical Exhibition in Philadelphia.

Office. By using the inventions of the earlier workers in wireless, improving them in detail and adapting them to his requirements, Marconi was able to build a practical working system. For a long time Marconi could not believe that he was the only one who had done this—he thought that many other alert scientists would be studying the problem and would easily accomplish the same things

he had. But no one had. Marconi was the first to apply Hertzian waves to signalling in such a manner that it could be made a commercial success.

The apparatus used today to send messages through space, whether the message is a voice, the sounds of music, television pictures, or telegraph signals, is in some ways similar to the old wireless equipment in principle. It makes use of Hertzian waves.

RADIO OPERATOR

The radio operator aboard ship is nicknamed "sparks." There is no more important member of the crew than the man who keeps a ship in touch with the world.

VACUUM TUBES

In modern radio, the sending of messages depends upon a miraculous vacuum tube. It does such wonderful things that it is sometimes likened to a modern Aladdin's lamp. The waves sent forth from a broadcasting station are produced by high-frequency alternating currents. They alternate hundreds of thousands of times per second. The currents are generated by circuits using vacuum tubes. You have no doubt seen the tubes used in home radios for receiving broadcast programs. The same sort of device, built on a larger scale and changed in some details, is also the means of sending messages. These tubes, they are often called "valves," are one of the most valuable and interesting creations of science. They look somewhat like

SAFETY AT SEA

The law requires that all passenger-carrying ships be equipped with radio. Many ships are equipped with both radiotelephone and radiotelegraph. They receive accurate time signals, frequent weather reports and can call for aid if necessary.

an electric-light bulb and, in fact, they were developed from the incandescent electric lamp.

VACUUM TUBES DEVELOPED FROM THE ELECTRIC LIGHT

In the early days of the old carbon-filament incandescent lamp which Edison created, the famous inventor noticed a peculiar action which he could not explain. When the lamps had been in use for a while, the inside of the glass bulb became darkened. Edison determined to find out what caused this action, for in the course of time they became so black that the amount of light was considerably diminished. He arranged a small metal plate inside a lamp bulb, near the filament but insulated from it, and was surprised to find that when this plate was connected to the positive terminal of a battery, a current would pass across the space between the plate and the filament. When the negative terminal of the battery was connected to the plate, no current would pass. Then when an alternating current was tried, only half of it would pass—that which flowed when the plate was positive. The arrangement was a sort of electrical valve. No one knew how to explain this action at that time and so for want of a better name, it was called the "Edison effect."

THE FLEMING VALVE

The first time that any practical use for the Edison effect was found was in 1904. Many years previously, Sir William Preece, while on a visit to the United States, obtained some of the lamps which Edison had built to demonstrate the Edison effect and carried them back to England with him. They fell into the hands of a young engineer named J. A. Fleming, who experimented with them.

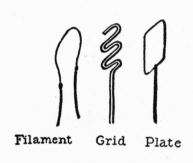

Filament   Grid   Plate

THE AUDION

The sketch shows the arrangement of the filament grid and plate in DeForest's invention which changed Fleming's valve into the much-improved audion.

For a long time, scientists had been looking for new types of detectors to use in receiving wireless telegraph signals, and with this in mind Fleming built an incandescent lamp with a little metal cylinder around the filament as a substitute for the small rectangular plate which Edison used. This was a great improvement on the original Edison arrangement and the new design proved to be a fairly good detector for receiving wireless telegraph signals. However, it remained for others to perfect it.

THE AUDION

In 1907, Doctor Lee De Forest conceived the idea of building an incandescent lamp with a plate inside like that which Edison had used, and in addition a small screen or perforated plate, called the grid, placed between the plate and the filament. He called his in-

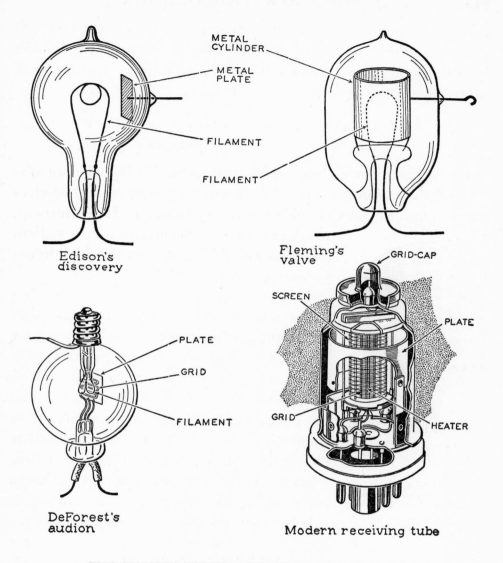

METAL
CYLINDER

METAL
PLATE

FILAMENT

FILAMENT

Edison's
discovery

Fleming's
valve

GRID-CAP

SCREEN

PLATE

PLATE

GRID

GRID

FILAMENT

HEATER

DeForest's
audion

Modern receiving tube

FOUR STAGES IN THE DEVELOPMENT OF THE RADIO TUBE

This useful device of modern electrical science began with Edison's discovery. Professor Fleming added a metal cylinder and called his device a valve. Lee De Forest added the grid and the valve became the audion. But it was a young college student, Edwin H. Armstrong of Columbia University, who found out how to make the audion generate alternating currents. Engineers of Western Electric Company and General Electric Company developed the modern tubes.

vention the *audion*. This arrangement proved to be a very much better detector of wireless signals than the "Fleming valve" and in addition could be used as an amplifier to magnify or increase weak electrical currents.

MODERN RADIO IS BASED UPON A DISCOVERY MADE BY A COLLEGE STUDENT

Up to this time nothing really very remarkable had been discovered about vacuum tubes. But in 1912 a young student of electrical engineering at Columbia University named E. H. Armstrong, who had been experimenting with the audion, made an astonishing discovery which revolutionized radio. Simply, it was this:

MICROPHONE

The mike, as it is called, used for broadcasting, is a specially built form of telephone transmitter sensitive enough to pick up sounds too feeble to be heard by a human ear.

In order to use one of the old Fleming valves, only one battery is necessary, that which supplies current to light the filament. Two batteries are required to operate a De Forest audion, one to light the filament and the other to supply current for what is called the plate circuit. There are three circuits in connection with an audion tube, the filament circuit, the grid circuit, and the plate circuit. Young Armstrong found that by properly connecting or "coupling," as it is called in this instance, the grid and plate circuits together, the audion would *become a generator of alternating currents of very high frequencies*. These currents alternated back and forth hundreds of thousands of times per second. This discovery of Armstrong's is called the *regenerative* or feedback circuit. It not only greatly improved the audion for receiving signals but gave it a brand-new use.

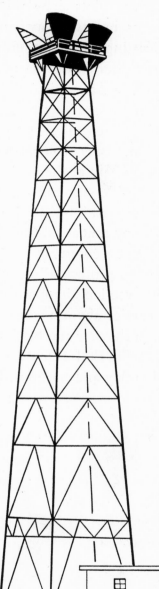

When high-frequency oscillations are sent into an antenna or aerial system, they send electromagnetic waves out into space. The high-frequency oscillations generated by an audion tube using Armstrong's discovery proved to be ideal for wireless telephony because they could be easily modulated or varied in accordance with the sounds of the voice when connected to a telephone transmitter or microphone.

The present-day system of broadcasting, telephoning across the ocean, and many other marvellous feats using the vacuum tube are the work of hundreds of men, but they all depend upon the discovery which young Armstrong made in a little bedroom laboratory in his home in Yonkers, New York.

RADIO RELAY MICROWAVE SYSTEMS

In addition to overhead and underground wires and coaxial cables, microwave radio relay systems provide broad pathways for telephone and telegraph

ANTENNA TOWER

messages, television programs and miscellaneous data signals. Radio waves are used in these radio relay systems but the waves differ greatly from those used for radio broadcasting in that their rate of vibration or frequency is very much higher. The most commonly used radio relay waves are about as long as a cigarette and millions of them go forth from the transmitting antenna every second. They are of the superhigh frequencies called microwaves and travel in a straight line like a beam of light. By concentrating the waves in a very narrow beam and aiming the beam at the horizon in the desired direction from the antenna, reliable communication is possible with stations as much as 200 miles apart. The tall antenna towers (see illustration) can be seen from many roads and highways.

The radio relay microwave system in most common use (also the oldest system) provides as many as 3,000 "protected" telephone circuits or five television channels in each direction along any given route. A more recently installed system carries about 11,000 telephone conversations. Television routes for both color and black-and-white programs, installed and maintained by the Bell Telephone system, consist of about 87,000 miles of radio relay and 6,000 miles of coaxial cable.

CHAPTER FIFTEEN

RADIO, TELEVISION, RADAR AND ELECTRONICS

THE word "electronics" has come into our language recently. Do you know what it means? It is the name of a branch of electrical science. In order to fully understand it let us go back to the latter part of the nineteenth century.

At that time, two scientists who were working independently of each other made the same discovery. The scientists were Sir William Crookes and Julius Plücker. Each was experimenting with a sausage-shaped glass tube fitted with two platinum electrodes: a cathode and an anode. The tube was connected to a mercury pump so that all but a very small amount of the air inside the tube could be pumped out. From time to time as the amount of air inside the tube was reduced, high voltage current from an induction coil was sent through the tube from electrode to electrode. At first, the current caused the tube to fill with a luminous glow. When the vacuum was carried to a higher degree, the whole tube did not become luminous. Part of it remained dark. When the pumping out process was carried to the highest degree possible, the dark space filled the entire tube, but the glass walls themselves became fluorescent with a strange greenish yellow light. What could account for this? To investigate further, Sir William put small pieces of metal in his tube between the cathode and anode. The metal pieces cast a sharp shadow in the fluorescence on the glass wall opposite the cathode. When a small metal paddle wheel was placed in front of the cathode and current was passed through the tube the wheel turned as if

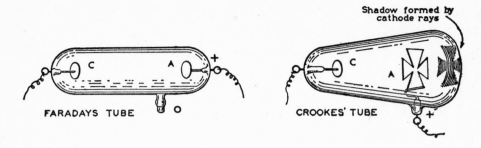

CATHODE–RAY TUBES

The left-hand sketch shows a tube similar to that used by Faraday. C is the cathode consisting of a platinum disk attached to a platinum wire hermetically (airtight) sealed in the end of the tube. The anode A is similar to the cathode. A small opening O in the wall of the tube permits a vacuum pump to be connected to evacuate the tube. The present-day laboratory version of Crookes' tube is illustrated by the right-hand sketch. The anode is a metal Maltese cross. When a high voltage current from an induction coil or static machine is applied to the anode and cathode, the large end of the tube emits a green glow. However, the Maltese cross intercepts the electrons and a shadow of the cross appears at the end of the tube.

something was striking against its paddles. Both Crookes and Plücker were correct in surmising that something which came from the negative electrode or cathode caused the fluorescence and turned the paddle wheel. They suggested that invisible rays were shot forth from the cathode and struck the walls of the tube with sufficient energy to cause the glass to fluoresce. "It is radiant matter," said Crookes, "which strikes the glass." Because the fluorescence was much greater near the cathode, the name cathode rays was adopted. It has since been proven that cathode rays do not exist in the same sense as light rays, but the term still persists and the name cathode-ray tube is applied to an important and useful type of vacuum tube used in laboratories and in television and radar.

ELECTRONS

A scientist named Jean Perrin, in 1895, definitely proved to the scientific world that the so-called "rays" coming from the cathode were actually tiny moving particles and that these particles carried a negative charge of electricity. Two years later, Sir Joseph John Thomson determined both the weight and the speed of the newly found particle. In 1897 a name was given the particle; it was called the "electron."

Electrons are the most elementary charge of negative electricity. The British physicist G. Johnstone Stoney first used the word electron in its modern sense to describe a fundamental particle of electricity. The movement of a stream of electrons is called an electric current. Electronics deals with the behavior of electrons.

ELECTRON TUBES

A tube which is used to control the flow of electrons in a circuit is called an electron tube. Radio tubes are one of the many types of electron tubes. A tube may be partly evacuated (all air removed), completely evacuated or it may be gas-filled; if it is used to control the flow of electrons in a circuit, it is an electron tube. Radio tubes, rectifier tubes, cathode-ray tubes, oscilloscopes, X-ray tubes and photo-electric tubes are all electron tubes.

The field of electronics embraces all apparatus employing electron tubes. Radio and television are the major branches of electronics. Included in its domain are radar, loran, talking-motion pictures, television, electronic computers, photo-electric cells, amplifiers, the recording and reproduction of sound, facsimile, public address systems, infra-red devices for seeing in the dark, X-rays, the electron microscope and the cyclotron used by nuclear physicists.

VACUUM-TUBE AMPLIFIERS

For many years scientists sought a means to strengthen or *amplify* the feeble currents in telephone circuits and radio receivers. Finally, the audion solved the problem. Used at first as a detector only, this three-element vacuum tube was found to be an excellent amplifier.

The word "amplifier" comes from two Latin words which mean "one or that which makes ample."

A very small amount of electrical energy fed to the grid of a three-electrode vacuum tube (some amplifier tubes have more than three electrodes) will produce considerable increase in the current flowing in the plate circuit of the tube. The tube can be used to magnify either voltage or amperage or both if necessary. Each amplifier tube and its circuit is called a stage. Several stages can be connected together and a great deal of amplification secured.

Modern radio receivers usually include at least two stages of amplification. One tube (detector) only is required to receive signals. The additional tubes in a receiver are amplifier tubes, employed to strengthen the signals. One or more of the tubes are connected so that they increase the strength of the currents in the antenna before they reach the detector. Such an arrangement is called a radio-frequency amplifier. Another amplifier of one or more stages then increases the strength of the signals after they have passed through the detector, adding sufficient energy to them to operate a loud-speaker. This amplifier which is connected to the speaker is an audio-frequency amplifier.

Before amplifiers were developed, radio messages were received with headphones. A detector alone does not supply enough energy to operate a loudspeaker. Amplifiers are used in radio, television and radar transmitters as well as in the receivers for these systems.

In the year 1915 the first transcontinental telephone line reaching from New York to San Francisco was put in operation. Until then it was impracticable to telephone more than 1,000 miles and that could be accomplished only by shouting into the transmitter. The tiny electrical impulses which carry the voice over telephone wires were lost in travelling greater distances. Vacuum-tube amplifiers made transcontinental telephony practical. In fact, no place on

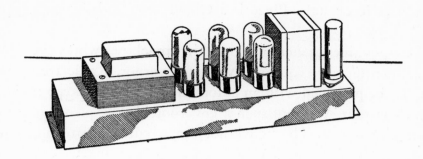

ELECTRONIC AMPLIFIERS

Electronic amplifiers employ one or more radio tubes or transistors to increase voltage, current or power. There are many types of amplifiers. An audio-frequency amplifier for use with a phonograph or public address system is illustrated above.

earth is now too far away to reach by telephone. Vacuum-tube amplifiers, known as "repeaters" in telephone language, are used to strengthen the voice currents. The buildings which shelter the repeaters are called repeater stations. Long-distance messages pass through several repeater stations. At each repeater station the voice currents are renewed and strengthened by the amplifying action of the repeater tube.

Amplifiers are equally invaluable in other fields. They are used in phonographs both for recording and playing records, in making and showing talking-motion pictures, in public address systems, in electrocardiographs, in sound detectors and in photo-electric apparatus.

PIEZO-ELECTRICITY

Certain crystals, among them quartz, Rochelle salt, tourmaline, topaz, fluorospar and sugar have a remarkable property. When squeezed or twisted they produce electricity. The electricity thus produced is called PIEZO-electricity and such crystals are called piezo-electric crystals. Piezo is a Greek word which means "pressure."

Clocks, engines, generators and other machines whose speed must be kept constant are equipped with a governor. Radio transmitters must also be provided with an automatic governor to keep their frequency constant. Without such a governor, the frequency of a radio station would shift. The "governor" in a radio-transmitting circuit is a piezo-electric crystal. Although the piece of quartz used for this purpose is called a crystal, it is not a whole crystal but only a section cut in the form of a flat plate.

When the quartz plate is placed between two metal electrodes to which an alternating current is applied, the quartz will vibrate and produce piezo-electricity. The frequency at which the quartz vibrates depends upon its thickness. Properly connected to a radio transmitter the quartz will keep the station at the same frequency. If it becomes necessary to change the frequency of the station, it is also necessary to change quartz crystals. Grinding and mounting quartz crystals is an important branch of the radio industry.

Piezo-electric crystals are used also in the construction of "crystal" microphones, telephone receivers and phonograph pickups. A crystal microphone consists of a pair of Rochelle salt crystals cemented together and mechanically connected to a diaphragm. When sound waves strike the diaphragm, the diaphragm vibrates and causes the crystals to vibrate and generate piezo-electricity. The piezo-electricity is fed into an amplifier connected to a radiophone or a broadcast transmitter.

PHONOGRAPHS AND PICKUPS

Previous to 1920, or thereabouts, music in the home was supplied by musicians, an automatic piano, a music box or a tinny-sounding phonograph which wore out records quickly.

In order to manufacture phonograph records in those days before electronics, the first step was to cut a wax master record. The record was cut by a sharp-pointed stylus attached to a small diaphragm. The diaphragm was attached to the smaller end of a horn or megaphone and was set into vibration by sound waves which entered the megaphone. The voice of a speaker or singer or music directed into the microphone produced sound waves which caused the diaphragm to vibrate and move the stylus. As the wax record revolved, the stylus moved back and forth and cut a wavy line in the wax surface. The wavy line was a recording of some but not all of the sounds which entered the megaphone. Sounds which were not within the range of the diaphragm or which were too weak did not move the diaphragm to cut the wax and were not recorded.

The next step was to electroplate the master record and from it make a metal master mold. From the master mold a number of production molds were then made and these were used to press out the records which reached the public through the record shops. The finished records each bore a sound groove or wavy line which was a faithful reproduction of that engraved in the original master record. The fault of these old records lay in the fact that many sound waves lacked sufficient energy to cut their impression in the master record and the master was consequently not a faithful record of the sounds it was intended to record.

The records were played on a turntable which revolved at the same speed as the master record turned when it was cut. A sharp needle attached to a mica diaphragm at the smaller end of a horn was placed in the sound groove. As the record turned, the needle followed the wavy line and as the needle moved back and forth it caused the mica diaphragm to move or vibrate. The vibrations of the diaphragm reproduced the sounds which originally made the wavy line on the wax record. The reproduction was similar to the original voice or music but not identical. It was squawky.

The music from the early broadcast receivers, although not so faithful as that from modern receivers, was superior to the music of the old phonographs. Consequently, the advent of broadcasting almost drove the phonograph and record companies out of business. However, electronics soon revived the industry.

Electronics brought a revolution in the method of making records and bringing forth sounds from them. The magic of amplification gave to records and phonographs the quality called fidelity. The sounds from present-day records, in so far as the ear can tell, are faithful reproductions of the original.

Today, in making a master record, the sounds to be recorded generate a tiny electric current. The fluctuations of the current keep in perfect step with the sounds. Nothing is missed. The current need do no work; it does not need the energy to push a stylus back and forth and cut wax in order to record the sounds which produced it. It merely controls an amplifier so that power, plenty of power, from the 120-volt lines and not the feeble energy of sound waves drives the cutting stylus back and forth. The result is a wavy line which is a faithful reproduction of the tiny fluctuations of voice or music. When a master record has been cut it is not difficult to make from it the master mold and the production molds for manufacturing.

Playing a modern record is the reverse of cutting it. Here again electronics has a role. The stylus or needle on a "pickup" wiggles as it follows the wavy groove and translates its motion into tiny electric currents. The currents control a vacuum-tube amplifier and it is the powerful output of this amplifier that drives the paper cone of the speaker in and out, faithfully reproducing the motion of the stylus in the groove on the record.

There are two types of pickups for translating the motion of a stylus into electric current. One is called a crystal pickup. It employs a piezo-electric crystal. The motion of the stylus twists the crystal slightly and generates a current. The other is called a variable

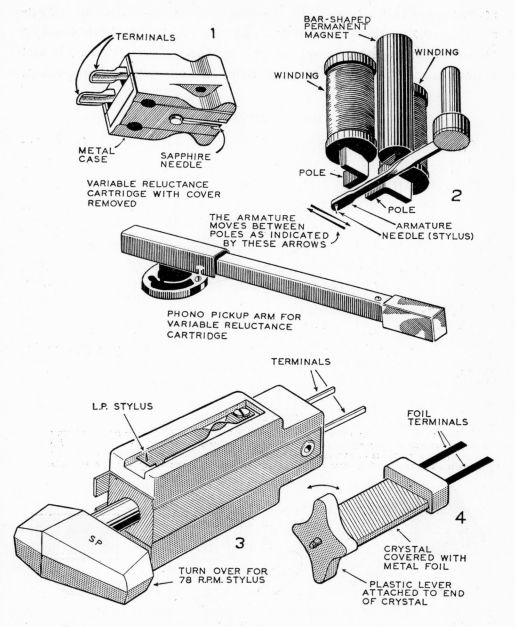

TERMINALS

1

BAR-SHAPED
PERMANENT
MAGNET

WINDING

WINDING

POLE

POLE

2

ARMATURE
NEEDLE (STYLUS)

METAL
CASE

SAPPHIRE
NEEDLE

VARIABLE RELUCTANCE
CARTRIDGE WITH COVER
REMOVED

THE ARMATURE
MOVES BETWEEN
POLES AS INDICATED
BY THESE ARROWS

PHONO PICKUP ARM FOR
VARIABLE RELUCTANCE
CARTRIDGE

TERMINALS

L.P. STYLUS

FOIL
TERMINALS

4

SP

3

TURN OVER FOR
78 R.P.M. STYLUS

CRYSTAL
COVERED WITH
METAL FOIL

PLASTIC LEVER
ATTACHED TO END
OF CRYSTAL

PHONOGRAPH PICKUPS

reluctance pickup. Essentially it consists of a small permanent magnet and two small coils of wire. The motion of the stylus changes the strength of the magnetism cutting through the two coils and generates a current which is then amplified and sent into a speaker.

THE ELECTRIC EYE

Photo-electric cell is the technical name for the very useful device popularly called an "electric eye." A photo-electric cell is sensitive to light. It will respond to changes in the strength of light a thousand times more rapidly than human eyes can and detect smaller changes. Photo-electric cells are employed as burglar alarms, to count people, vehicles or other objects which pass a certain spot, to bring elevators level with the floor when they stop, to control automatic machines and for dozens of other purposes. One of the most important uses is in talking-motion pictures.

There are several varieties of photo-electric cell. The most common varieties are the selenium, silicon, cadmium-sulfide and alkaline types.

PHOTO–ELECTRIC CELLS

The cell at the left is an International Rectifier Corporation B2M experimenter selenium cell. It will generate 0.3 to 0.4 volts and 2 milliamperes in sunlight. The cadmium-sulfide cell has a resistance of approximately 1,000,000 ohms in total darkness and a few hundred ohms in sunlight. Many sizes of the type of selenium cell shown at the right are available.

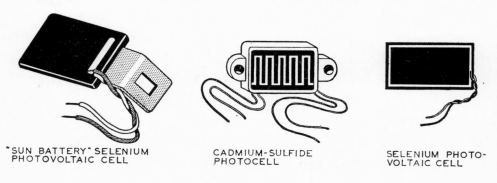

"SUN BATTERY" SELENIUM   CADMIUM-SULFIDE   SELENIUM PHOTO-
PHOTOVOLTAIC CELL   PHOTOCELL   VOLTAIC CELL

Alexander Graham Bell, the famous inventor of the telephone, and an associate named Sumner Tainter, made the first photo-electric cell. They used selenium in its construction. Their purpose was to develop a light-sensitive device which could be used in the construction of a "photophone," a form of telephone, which employed a beam of light in place of wires to carry a conversation. They succeeded in building a photophone which would transmit and receive telephone messages for several hundred feet.

Selenium is a chemical element belonging to the sulfur group. The selenium used in making cells is carefully processed and prepared to permit electrons to be freed by light. Selenium contains many electrons but these are held tightly in place unless the selenium is illuminated. When selenium is illuminated, the light activates the electrons and they will travel through an electrical circuit. The movement of electrons through a circuit constitutes an electrical circuit.

To make a selenium cell, a thin layer of the element is spread on a small iron plate. A wire lead is attached to the iron plate. A second wire lead is connected to the surface of the selenium film. A selenium cell has two amazing properties. One is the fact that when light strikes the cell, a tiny electric current is generated. The first commercial use for light-generated electricity from a selenium cell is the light meter used to indicate the correct exposure setting for cameras. The light meter consists of a selenium cell connected to a sensitive galvanometer. When light strikes the cell a tiny current is generated and causes the pointer on the meter to move. The needle moves farther when the light is bright than it does when the light is dim.

The second amazing property of a selenium cell is the fact that its resistance to the flow of an electric current is much less when the cell is in the light than when it is in darkness. If a selenium cell is placed in a circuit in series with a battery and a sensitive relay an electric current can flow only by passing through the selenium cell. When the cell is in darkness its resistance is so high that not enough current will flow to operate the relay. But if light strikes the cell, enough current will flow to close the relay. A bell, motor, horn, door-opener, counter, valve, switch and many other mechanisms can be connected to the relay so that they will be stopped or started by a beam of light. Or, by changing the position of one of the relay contacts these devices can be stopped or started by an interruption of the light.

A cell made from cadmium-sulfide changes its resistance when removed from darkness and into the light but does not generate an electric current. When the cadmium-sulfide is illuminated, its resistance drops to a low value; when in darkness, it increases to millions of ohms. By connecting a cadmium-sulfide cell in series with a current supply and a relay, the circuit becomes a light-controlled switch with innumerable uses.

The alkaline type of photo-electric cell is more sensitive than a selenium cell. In general appearance, it resembles the common radio tubes used in an ordinary radio receiver and consequently is called a phototube. There is more than one type of phototube. One of the most sensitive is constructed so that the inside surface of the glass bulb is covered with a thin coating of silver except for one small spot where the glass is left transparent so that light can enter the tube. Over the silver tube is a thin film of potassium hydrate. The silver coating forms one electrode of the cell and is connected to a contact pin on the base. In the center of the tube is a wire loop or a straight piece of wire insulated from the silver and potassium coatings. This wire is the second electrode and it also is connected to a contact pin on the base.

Light which enters the tube through the transparent window and strikes the potassium coating generates a feeble electric current.

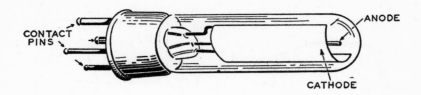

PHOTOTUBE

Phototubes are constructed so that the action of light striking a light-sensitive film of potassium or caesium releases electrons. In one type of phototube the light-sensitive film is on the inside surface of the glass envelope. In the phototube illustrated above, the light-sensitive film is on the surface of a curved metal plate (the cathode). The anode is a straight piece of wire centrally located in the envelope. The anode and the cathode are both electrically connected to contact pins on the base.

If the electrodes of the cell are connected to an amplifier the current generated in the cell is greatly magnified and the most minute changes in the intensity of the light entering the cell may be detected. Talking movies and wirephoto and radiophoto systems employ alkaline photo-electric cells.

SOLAR CELLS

When space scientists first became interested in building a satellite to orbit the earth and send radio reports back, they faced the problem of a dependable current supply. Dry cells would become exhausted after a few days or weeks of operation. Storage cells would require frequent recharging.

The "solar cell" was the answer. A battery of solar cells (cells which convert sunlight directly into electricity) would recharge a storage battery when the satellite sped around the sunlit side of the earth. For example, the Tiros satellite which takes pictures of the earth for weather forecasting is powered by sunlight falling on panels made up of solar cells. These panels supply enough current to keep

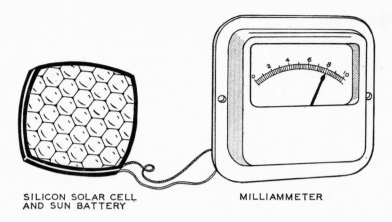

SILICON SOLAR CELL   MILLIAMMETER
AND SUN BATTERY

SOLAR CELL

This is an International type S1M silicon solar cell connected to a milliameter. The cell
has an approximate output in sunlight of 0.3 to 0.45 volts and 10 to 16 milliamperes.

the storage batteries fully recharged and the electronic equipment
working.

Scientifically, cells which convert sunlight directly into an electric current are known as photo-voltaic cells. Selenium cells are
photo-voltaic cells. But another type of cell, the one used in satellites,
is a much more efficient photo-voltaic cell. It is made of silicon, the
most common element found on our earth. Silicon is the principal
constituent of sand. The process required to prepare silicon for making solar cells is relatively expensive and makes silicon cells more
costly than selenium cells.

TALKING-MOTION PICTURES

The electronic amplifier, the photo-electric cell and ingenuity
brought us the modern talking-motion picture. Perhaps you have
seen a piece of "talking film" and noticed the jagged black line
alongside the pictures. This is the sound track. Like the wavy groove
in a phonograph record, this jagged line was produced by sounds.

In it may be stored the music of an opera, or the speech of a great man. The sound track does not discriminate; it will store any sounds.

To bring forth the music and speech recorded in the sound track, an electric light is placed on one side of the film. The light is focused in a tiny beam so that a small spot only strikes the film. A photo-electric cell is placed on the opposite side of the film and all the light which reaches the cell must pass through the sound track. As the film moves through the picture projector, the amount of light which reaches the cell varies in accordance with the speech, music or other sounds recorded on the track. The photo-electric cell produces an electric current which varies correspondingly. These currents are sent through an amplifier so that they are strengthened sufficiently to operate a loudspeaker. Thus a picture film is made to talk.

FACSIMILE-PICTURES BY WIRE AND RADIO

By means of facsimile, photographs, drawings or printed pages made in San Francisco, London or distant lands can appear a few hours later in a New York newspaper. Facsimile is made possible by the electric eye. Of course a photograph cannot actually be sent in the sense of being transported by wire or radio. But AN EXACT COPY of a photograph, drawing or of a written or printed page can be produced at a distant point in a matter of minutes. The original remains at the transmitting station.

Watch the process: A photograph to be transmitted is clamped to a revolving cylinder which makes 100 complete revolutions per minute. During the same length of time, while the cylinder is re-volving, it also moves sideways half an inch. A strong beam of light which forms a tiny spot $\frac{1}{200}$-inch square is focused on the pho-tograph. As the photograph slowly revolves and at the same time moves sidewise, the entire surface of the picture is searched or scanned by the tiny spot of light. The amount of light reflected back from the small illuminated spot on the photograph varies according to whether the color of the area which the beam strikes is black, gray or white. A white area reflects the most light, a black area reflects the least. This fluctuating reflected light is gathered by a hollow mirror and focused on a photo-electric cell. The cell produces an electric current which fluctuates with the strength of the light. The current is too weak to send directly out over a long line or to modulate a radio transmitter, so it goes next through an amplifier and is greatly strengthened. Then it is sent out over the telephone or telegraph lines or into a powerful radio transmitter.

At the receiving office, the current coming in over the wires (or from a radio detector if the picture is sent via radio) first passes into an amplifier, then through a device called a light valve. This ingenious "gadget" is a tiny duralumin ribbon stretched across a small opening in the magnetic field of a small coil of wire. A strong beam of light from an incandescent lamp is directed at the opening in the coil. The fluctuating current of the "picture message" passes through the duralumin ribbon and causes the ribbon to move and vary the amount of light which comes out of the opening. The light which comes out of the opening is focused on a light-sensitive photographic film mounted on a revolving cylinder. The cylinder revolves and moves sidewise at the same rate of speed as the cylinder at the transmitting station. The fluctuating light from the light valve leaves its impression on the sensitive film. When the latter is developed (like an ordinary photograph) the picture appears. The film can then be used as a negative to make prints and halftone engravings for the printing presses.

THE CATHODE-RAY OSCILLOSCOPE

This instrument is to the engineer as the X-ray machine is to the physician. It permits the observer to see what is occurring in an electric circuit. Its moving electron beam traces patterns on a fluorescent screen which mean nothing to the layman but tell a complete story to the trained technician. An oscilloscope is practically instantaneous in its action. Variations in voltage occurring at rates of millions of times per second become visible on the screen and may be carefully studied. Oscilloscopes are used in thousands of laboratories. The picture tubes of television and the screen tubes of radar receivers are cathode-ray oscilloscope tubes.

A cathode-ray oscilloscope consists of a special type of cathode-ray tube plus its auxiliary circuits. The tube dates back to some experiments with vacuum tubes which Michael Faraday conducted about 1865. However, it remained largely a mere laboratory curiosity until it was improved by Dr. Allan B. Dumont. In 1931, when he was still a very young man, Dumont began research and development work on the cathode-ray tube. He continued his experiments for several years and the result, about 1938, was a tube which operated on the same principles as the present day "scopes" and picture tubes used in radar, television and laboratory work.

Technical men who use the cathode-ray oscilloscope in their daily work shorten its three-word name to "oscilloscope" and "scope."

An oscilloscope tube is a more or less pear-shaped glass tube or bulb containing:

1. An electron gun
2. A fluorescent screen
3. A device for focusing the electron beam in a small spot on the fluorescent screen
4. A means of deflecting or moving the electron beam. This part of the oscilloscope may be either inside or outside the tube

The electron gun consists of a heater and a cathode. The cathode is treated with a chemical which produces electrons when heated.

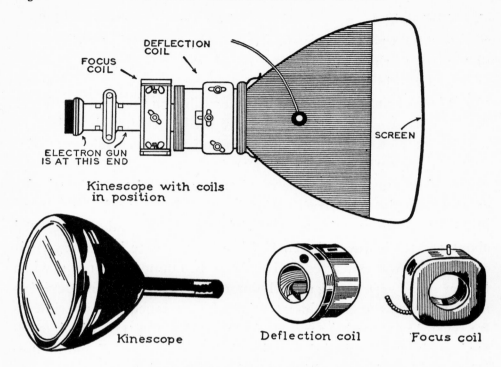

FOCUS COIL

DEFLECTION COIL

ELECTRON GUN IS AT THIS END

SCREEN

Kinescope with coils in position

Kinescope

Deflection coil

Focus coil

KINESCOPE OR TELEVISION PICTURE TUBE

The kinescope is a cathode-ray oscilloscope built for the special purpose of producing television pictures. The scopes used for radar and laboratory work are similar in principle but smaller. The fluorescent materials used to form the screen are varied to make a screen which best suits the purpose of a tube. The deflection coil moves the electron beam.

The gun is built into the neck of the tube. It is called a gun because it generates and "shoots" a beam of electrons at the fluorescent screen at the opposite end of the tube.

The fluorescent screen is a thin coating of one or more of the chemicals called phosphors. Wherever the electron beam strikes the screen, the phosphor glows.

There are two types of oscilloscope tubes. The difference between them is in the means used to focus and to move or deflect the electron beam. When the tube is in operation, the electron beam may be moved up or down or sidewise. In "scopes" made for laboratory work and certain radar devices, the electron beam is focused and deflected by electrical charges applied to four metal plates built in the tube. In the scopes used in television receivers, the electron beam is focused and deflected by four electromagnets outside the tube.

RADIOTELEGRAPHY AND RADIOTELEPHONY

Radio enables one part of the world to know instantly what the rest of the world is doing. By the magic of a vacuum tube, pictures, words, music and telegraph signals can be sent into space and picked up again thousands of miles away. As a result, you know much more about what is going on in the world than your grandparents did at your age.

The radio waves which carry the signals of radiotelegraphy, radiotelephony, television, radar and facsimile are termed carrier waves by radio engineers. Carrier waves are produced by sending high-frequency alternating currents into an antenna. The high-frequency currents are generated by a vacuum-tube oscillator.[1]

Carrier waves are given their message by an interesting process called modulation which varies the waves so that the variations correspond to the signal or message. There are two basic methods of modulation. A carrier wave can be modulated by varying either the strength or the frequency of the wave.

Modulating a wave by varying the strength of the wave in accordance with the signals it is to carry is amplitude modulation, abbreviated AM. This is the older and more common method.

Modulating a wave by varying its frequency in accordance with the signals it is to carry is frequency modulation, abbreviated FM Static does not interfere with FM signals.

---

[1] An oscillator consists of one or more vacuum tubes connected in a circuit which is arranged so that high-frequency alternating currents are produced.

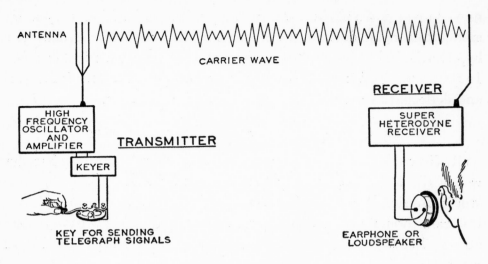

ANTENNA

CARRIER WAVE

RECEIVER

HIGH
FREQUENCY
OSCILLATOR
AND
AMPLIFIER

TRANSMITTER

SUPER
HETERODYNE
RECEIVER

KEYER

KEY FOR SENDING
TELEGRAPH SIGNALS

EARPHONE OR
LOUDSPEAKER

RADIOTELEGRAPHY

By comparing this diagram with the two which follow you will notice that the basic difference between radiotelegraphy, radiotelephony and television lies in the method of modulating or impressing the signals on the carrier wave.

The telephone is a good example of a modulation process. When a telephone is in use, a "carrier current" flows through the circuit. Speaking into the telephone transmitter modulates or varies the strength of the carrier current. The fluctuations in the current cause the diaphragm of a telephone receiver to vibrate and produce sound waves.

The present-day radiotelegraph transmitter consists of an oscillator, an antenna, a key and a modulator. The modulator of a radio telegraph transmitter is usually termed a keyer. The keyer is controlled by an ordinary telegraph key or by a tape-operated machine when messages are sent at high speed. The key and keyer modulate the carrier wave by breaking it up into groups corresponding to the dots and dashes of the telegraph code. When the waves strike the antenna of the receiving station, they produce small high-frequency currents in little groups corresponding to the dot and dash signals. In order to produce audible signals, the currents in the antenna are passed through a radio-frequency amplifier, tuner and detector. The amplifier strengthens the antenna currents and the tuner prevents interference from other transmitters which may be operating at the same time within range of the receiver. The detector is necessary in order to change the high-frequency alternating currents into direct currents which are then boosted or amplified by an audio-frequency amplifier. An earphone or loudspeaker changes the direct currents into sound and makes the signals audible.

A radiotelephone transmitter is quite similar to a radiotelegraph transmitter. The same type of oscillator and antenna is employed.

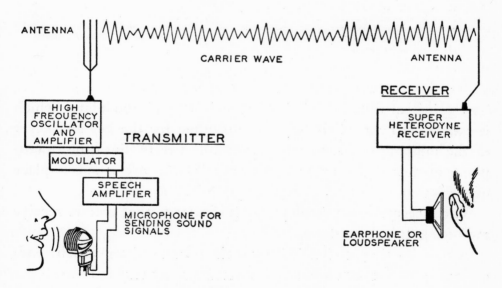

ANTENNA

CARRIER WAVE

ANTENNA

RECEIVER

HIGH FREQUENCY OSCILLATOR AND AMPLIFIER

TRANSMITTER

SUPER HETERODYNE RECEIVER

MODULATOR

SPEECH AMPLIFIER

MICROPHONE FOR SENDING SOUND SIGNALS

EARPHONE OR LOUDSPEAKER

THE PRINCIPAL OF RADIOTELEPHONY

Radio engineers often draw a square or rectangle (called "a block") to represent intricate apparatus or machinery. This illustration, the one immediately preceding it and the one following it are "block" diagrams in which the modulators, etc., are represented as rectangles. Diagrams showing all the details would be too complicated to have much meaning to anyone but a radio engineer. A block diagram is somewhat like an architect's floor plan for a house. Squares or rectangles show the size, shape and location of the rooms without showing the details of construction.

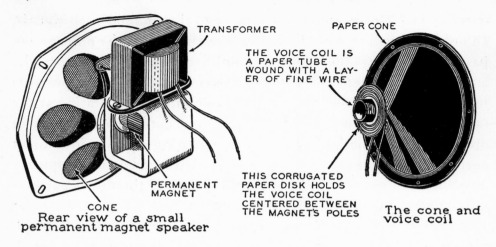

TRANSFORMER

PAPER CONE

THE VOICE COIL IS
A PAPER TUBE
WOUND WITH A LAY-
ER OF FINE WIRE

PERMANENT
MAGNET

THIS CORRUGATED
PAPER DISK HOLDS
THE VOICE COIL
CENTERED BETWEEN
THE MAGNET'S POLES

CONE

Rear view of a small
permanent magnet speaker

The cone and
voice coil

THE VOCAL CORDS OF THE RADIO RECEIVER

A loudspeaker converts electrical currents into sound waves of sufficient volume to be heard by a group of people. The waves are produced by the motion of a paper cone. The cone is moved by an electromagnetic winding, called the voice coil, attached to the apex of the cone. The voice coil is supported in a magnetic field provided by a permanent magnet in the smaller sizes of loudspeaker used in portable and table model receivers. The transformer or coupling coils mounted on the back of the speaker connects the voice coils to the audio amplifier.

The principal difference is in the modulator. A modulator which is controlled by a microphone is substituted for the key and keyer of the radiotelegraph. Speech and music directed into the microphone modulate the carrier wave in accordance with sounds in place of the dots and dashes of the telegraph code.

The receiver for radiotelephony is similar to that used to receive radiotelegraph signals.

A broadcasting station is a radiophone transmitter which sends out regular programs for public entertainment and is licensed for that purpose only. The regulations under which a broadcasting station operates forbid its use for sending personal messages.

Ships at sea and telephone subscribers across the ocean can be reached from any Bell System phone. If you make such a call or are called, your phone is connected to a powerful radiophone transmitter and to a sensitive radio receiver, both of which are owned and operated by the American Telegraph and Telephone Company.

Personal or business telegraph messages are sent abroad or to ships at sea via radiotelegraph stations owned and operated by RCA Communications and other radio communications companies licensed by the Federal Government.

TELEVISION

In television, the tiny invisible electron annihilates time and space and brings us a moving picture of sporting contests, dramas, concerts, conventions, stage appearances and other events currently happening in distant places. The scenes and sounds sent forth from a television station are carried by the same kind of carrier waves that are employed to carry the messages of the radiotelegraph and radiophone. There is only this difference: the television waves are shorter.

The long carrier waves used in broadcasting follow the curvature of the earth to a great extent, but the shorter waves of television do not. Television waves behave like light waves in one respect; they move straight out from the transmitting antenna. They miss receiving antennas which are beyond the horizon. When they encounter buildings or hills they cast "shadows" which eliminate or weaken signals behind the obstruction. Often, the short waves are reflected from buildings, tanks, hills, towers, etc. Reflected waves cause secondary images or "ghosts" in a television receiver. The antenna of a TV transmitter is erected as high as possible in order to obtain the maximum range and reduce ghosts and shadows. For that reason several television stations in New York City broadcast from antennas located on the tower of the 1,250-foot Empire State Building. The red aircraft-warning beacon on the top of the antenna tower is 1,467 feet above Fifth Avenue. Projecting from the four sides of the antenna tower is a group of steel wave-radiating elements called dipoles which make up the antenna for each station.

The portion of a television station's equipment which picks up and broadcasts sound is the AUDIO part and is exactly like the equipment used for the same purpose in a radio broadcasting transmitter. Similarly the part of a television receiver which reproduces sound is the AUDIO portion and it is exactly like the common broadcast receiver except that it is built to tune in short wavelengths.

The visual portion of a television program is broadcast and received by VIDEO apparatus. The video transmitter differs from a broadcast transmitter only in the fact that light variations, instead of sound variations, modulate the carrier waves. The waves are given their picture signals by a modulator connected to a television camera. The camera has a lens like the lens in an ordinary camera but there the similarity ends. There is no film in the camera and the scene which comes in through the lens is focused instead on the screen of a special electron tube about 17 inches long. Usually, the tube is the type known as the Image Orthicon.

Like an oscilloscope tube, the image orthicon has a screen at one end and an electron gun at the other. However, the screen is not a fluorescent screen. It is composed of thousands of tiny spots coated with a light-sensitive chemical which gives off electrons when struck by light. The picture which the camera lens focuses on the screen is small, usually about 1¼-inch wide and ⅞-inch high. The dots covered by the lighter portions of a picture shoot out more electrons than the dots within the darker areas. The electrons shoot out from the dots on this screen to a second screen called the target. When the camera is in operation the target is continuously searched or scanned in a definite and orderly manner by an electron beam shot from the electron gun. The beam sweeps across the target and back

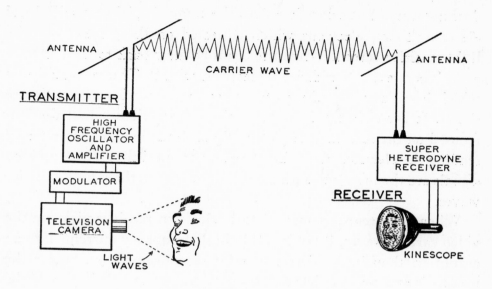

TELEVISION

This diagram illustrates the video portion only of a television transmitter and receiver. The audio apparatus is like that used in radiotelephony.

again in somewhat the same manner that our eyes move from left to right and back again when reading a page in a book. The beam starts at the left side of the target and sweeps across to the right side. Almost instantly it jumps back to the left and is ready to repeat the process. The beam moves infinitely faster than the human eye. It sweeps back and forth 525 times in scanning the target from top to bottom and scans the whole target 30 times per second. This rapid repetition is necessary so that a series of complete scannings blend and appear to our eyes like a single picture in the same way that the successive pictures of a motion picture film blend during projection.

The electron beam shot at the target by the electron gun bounces back from the target to a metal plate called the collector plate. The number of electrons in the beam shot at the target from the gun does not vary. But when it strikes the target it picks up additional electrons there, electrons which collected on the target from the light sensitive screen. When the beam bounces back to the collector plate it carries these additional electrons with it. The reflected beam which is collected on the plate has consequently become a picture signal. It is an electronic reproduction of the picture that the lens focused on the screen. The picture signal is made much stronger by sending the electrons from the plate into an amplifier. The amplified signals are then fed into a modulator which gives them to the carrier waves.

When an antenna connected to a television receiver picks up the video carrier waves, it sends feeble high-frequency currents into an amplifier, then into a detector and a second amplifier. So far the process is exactly like that employed to receive sound signals. If the signals were sound or audio signals they would next go to a loud-speaker so that they could be heard. But since the video signals are to produce a picture they go instead to a cathode-ray tube, a special oscilloscope tube made expressly for television receivers. The large end of this pear-shaped tube is a fluorescent screen. This is the screen of the receiver on which you see the pictures. At the small end of the tube is an electron gun. An electron beam scans the screen in perfect step with the electron beam in the image orthicon at the transmitter. Wherever the beam strikes the fluorescent screen, the screen gives off light. Since the beam of electrons fluctuates in strength exactly in step with the reflected beam in the camera tube it makes some spots on the screen brighter than others. The result is a picture in light on the fluorescent screen just like the picture that came through the camera lens and was focused on the camera screen. The picture at the television receiver consists of 525 lines of light and dark repeated 30 times a second. The 525 lines are traced on the screen so quickly that they appear as a whole picture and the 30 pictures a second appear as a moving picture because eyes do not function rapidly enough to see the intervals between.

COAXIAL CABLES

Frequently several television or broadcasting stations are connected together in order to send out the same program simultaneously. A group of stations so connected is called a network. One of the advantages of a radio or of a television network is its very large audience. The greater the number of listeners, the more a sponsor can afford to spend for a program.

The station in a network where a program originates is known as the "key" station. The key station of an AM radio network sends its program over telephone wires to the other stations of the network. But ordinary telephone wires cannot be used for transmitting the audio and video signals from a key television station. In order to show the same program at the same time, the stations in a television network are connected by coaxial cables or microwave relay. The cost of laying a coaxial cable underground from one city to another is too great for the television industry to make the investment. Therefore the cables are installed and owned by the American Telegraph and Telephone Company and the television stations pay tolls for their use.

A coaxial cable is a copper tube with a copper wire suspended in it. The name coaxial was adopted because the center or axis of the wire coincides with the center or axis of the tube. The wire inside the tube carries the signal; the tube keeps the signal from leaking away.

A. T. and T.'s coaxial cables run underground between cities. The cables consist of eight copper tubes bound together around a small telephone cable and enclosed in a protective lead sheath. Each one of the tubes has a copper wire suspended inside it. The

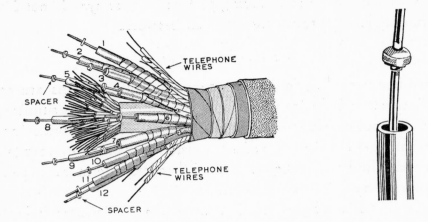

NEW 3–INCH THROUGHWAY FOR TELEPHONE CONVERSATIONS, DATA SIGNALS AND TELEVISION PROGRAMS

This cable now being placed underground from the East to the West Coast is the largest capacity telephone cable ever made. It contains 12 coaxial cables and a large number of telephone wires. Its coaxial units (numbered 1 to 12 in the illustration) can carry 11,160 telephone conversations at the same time. The new cable will provide additional alternate coast-to-coast telephone circuits and thus assure uninterrupted communications under all conditions.

    The right-hand sketch will help to explain a coaxial cable. It shows how the center conductor runs along the axis of the cable separated and insulated from the latter by plastic washers.

wires are held in the center of the tubes and insulated from them by ceramic spacer disks. The single wire conductor inside each tube can carry one television program and approximately 600 telephone conversations simultaneously. Only six of the tubes and conductors are usually in active service. Two are kept in reserve for emergencies. Each coaxial cable is able to carry six television programs and 3,500 telephone conversations simultaneously.

    Flexible coaxial cables are used in television studios to connect the camera to the transmitter. Flexibility is secured by replacing the copper tube with a woven copper shield and by using a stranded copper wire instead of a solid wire. Instead of using ceramic dielectric disks to insulate the copper wire from the copper sheath, the wire is covered with a thick layer of the plastic called polyethylene.

RADAR, THE GREAT DETECTIVE

When Japanese airplanes attacked the United States fleet at anchor in Pearl Harbor on that never-to-be-forgotten Sunday morning of December 7, 1941, the news reports told that a new electrical device had detected the presence of the Japanese carrier-based planes when they were still half an hour away. Censorship was clamped down immediately after this fragmentary mention of the electrical device and the public heard little or nothing more about it until Japan had sued for peace. Then it became known that the Japanese planes had been detected and located before they reached Pearl Harbor by means of radar.

During the war years marvellous improvements were made in radar. More was spent on radar by the United States Government than on the atomic bomb. Why is radar so important that several billion dollars were spent on radar equipment? The answer is because radar, more than any single development since the airplane, changed the face of warfare. Radar can see many times farther than the human eye can and radar's ability to see is relatively unaffected by darkness, rain, fog or smoke. Radar is the great detective of modern warfare. One of the greatest weapons of warfare is surprise, and surprise is usually achieved by concealment. Warships and airplanes once could approach in darkness, in clouds or in the glare of the sun and their presence would be unknown. But where there is radar, the concealment formerly afforded by darkness, fog, clouds, smokescreens or the glare of the sun simply does not exist.

It was radar, together with the shortwave radiotelephone, which enabled the Royal Air Force to defeat the German air blitz of England in 1940 and thereby stop the invasion of that island which Hitler had planned. It was only because of radar's aid that the German U-boats were defeated. A story of radar's contributions toward winning the war for the Allies would fill volumes.

Radar is an APPLICATION OF RADIO which detects the presence of objects, determines their range and direction and recognizes their character. Its principle is more easily understood if you bear in mind that all waves, whether they are light, sound, water or radio waves are reflected back when they meet an obstruction. A flashlight and a mirror on the wall of a darkened room will enable you to demonstrate reflected waves. Hold the flashlight so that its beam of light strikes the mirror and a beam of light will be reflected back. If you stand

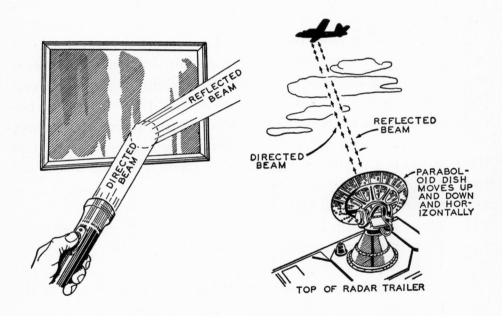

RADAR

A radar station sends out radio waves in the form of a beam which can be pointed in any direction like the beam of light from a flashlight. In the same way that a mirror struck by a beam of light from a flashlight reflects it back, so an object struck by a radar beam reflects it back to the transmitter. Noting the direction of the beam and measuring the time which elapses between sending a signal and the arrival of the echo or reflected beam indicates the exact location of a reflecting object even though it may be hidden by clouds or darkness or be beyond human vision.

directly in front of the mirror and direct the light beam toward it at eye level, the reflected light waves will travel back to your eyes.

Objects are detected by radar by directing a beam of extremely high-frequency radio waves over a region to be searched. When the beam strikes a reflecting object waves are reflected back and picked up by a sensitive radio receiver located near the transmitter. Such an echo signal from the receiver indicates the presence of an object or target.

The U. S. Navy coined the word radar as an abbreviation for "Radio Detection And Ranging." The word does not refer to a single instrument. A radar installation may be a comparatively small hundred-pound collection of instruments in an airplane; it may be an installation which fills a large trailer truck; it may be a couple of water-tight boxes and a slight bulge in the short mast of a PT boat; it may be tons of electronic equipment installed on a carrier or battleship; or it may be a sprawling collection of shacks and trucks requiring a whole company of men for its operation.

Most radar installations are composed of the following four units:

1. A radio transmitter
2. A sensitive radio receiver
3. A cathode-ray oscilloscope
4. An antenna which focuses the waves sent out by the transmitter into a beam and directs the beam

A radar's transmitter and receiver more often than not have a common antenna. In appearance a radar antenna bears little resemblance to the familiar antennas erected on housetops for receiving television and broadcasting programs. It may consist of two short metal rods bent at right angles, known as a dipole, which are set in the center of a large bowl-shaped metal reflector (popularly called a "dish" in radar slang) or it may consist of a number of dipoles mounted on a framework, the whole "array," as it is called, having much resemblance to a huge bedspring. In addition to these two types, there are other styles of radar antennas. All radars have one thing in common: they are movable so that their beam of radio waves can be made to search the land, sea and skies like the beam of a searchlight.

When in operation, a radar transmitter actually sends out waves only a very small part of the time. It sends the waves in intense bursts of short duration called pulses. The pulses may be only a millionth of a second long. During the interval between pulses—a few thousandths of a second—the antenna is disconnected from the transmitter and connected to the receiver. Between pulses, the receiver is working and any signals that it receives are echoes of the pulses, echoes reflected back from any objects which the pulses strike. The nearest objects send back echoes which reach the receiver very soon after the receiver pulse is finished. Those farther away send back echoes which arrive later than the echoes from nearby objects. The pulses travel outward from the antenna and the echoes travel back with the speed of light, namely, 186,000 miles per second or 328 yards each millionth of a second. The time between the transmission of a pulse and the reception of its echo measures the distance of the object reflecting back the echo. That object may be a ship, an airplane, a building or a mountain. An object 2,000 yards away gives an echo only twelve millionths of a second after the pulse occurred and one of the instruments connected to the receiver indicates that fact. The exact measurement of such extremely small intervals of time in radar is one of the technical triumphs of modern science. It is accomplished with the aid of a cathode-ray oscilloscope (a "scope" in radar slang). The returning echo picked up by a radar receiver produces a visual signal. It is seen, not heard, as are the signals picked up by the common radio receiver. Across the fluorescent screen of the scope there is normally a thin straight line of light. When pulses sent out by the radar transmitter are reflected back they produce a hump in the line or a bright spot. A hump or a bright spot is called a "pip" (radar slang for target indication). The strongest pip is produced when the beam of outgoing pulses is pointed directly at the target. The bearing of the antenna then indicates the bearing of the target. The screen of the scope is marked so that the position of the pip on the screen indicates the distance of the object that caused the pip. The operator watching the scope can read a range scale down to a few yards. This information may then be used to point anti-aircraft guns, aim a warship's guns or artillery, set the course of a bomber or direct a fighter plane.

In directing Army anti-aircraft fire, the radar antenna moves automatically so that it always points at the target plane without help from the radar operator and the guns follow automatically.

One of the most remarkable radar developments is called PPI, these letters being an abbreviation of Plan Position Indicator. In

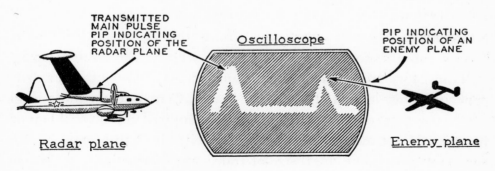

TRANSMITTED MAIN PULSE PIP INDICATING POSITION OF THE RADAR PLANE

Oscilloscope

PIP INDICATING POSITION OF AN ENEMY PLANE

Radar plane

Enemy plane

RADAR SCOPE

The simplest radar scope is the Type "A" illustrated above. A peak or "pip" in the luminous line on the screen of the scope indicates a possible target. The distance between the main pip indicating the position of the radar set and the pip indicating a plane or ship gives the range in yards.

TRANSISTORS

The five transistors at the left are types used in radio receivers, small amplifiers, etc. That at the right is a "power" transistor able to handle 40 watts when mounted on a suitable heat sink to dissipate the heat.

this device, the radar echoes are caused to draw a map in light on the screen of the oscilloscope. A bomber flying high above the clouds in darkness but equipped with PPI has at all times a map of the earth directly below. Rivers, harbors, cities and ships are easily distinguished.

TRANSISTORS—WHAT THEY ARE AND CAN DO

In 1948, W. H. Brattain and John Bardeen, scientists employed by the Bell Telephone Laboratories, made a priceless discovery. They discovered that a tiny wafer of the element germanium can perform many of the functions of a radio tube. It can serve as a detector, amplifier, oscillator and relay in radio and electronic circuits. It is small, rugged and efficient. This new device is called a TRANSISTOR. The word was coined from "transit resistor," the temporary name bestowed by the scientists who helped to develop it.

Transistors are much smaller than electron tubes of equivalent capacity. They have no filament or heater. Consequently there is no "A" battery or source of heating current required and no problem of burnout. If not mistreated, a transistor will give continuous service for many years. The small size of transistors has made it possible to build the popular pocket radios, small recorders and miniature "walkie-talkies." The uses for transistors in electronics are practically unlimited. A transistor can perform as a valve, a switch, a relay, a detector, an amplifier and an oscillator. They are an essential part of many varieties of radio transmitters, radio receivers, hearing aids, phonographs, tape recorders, automatic telephone exchanges, digital computers, industrial control systems and telemetering transmitters and receivers for satellites.

There are several types of transistors and they all may be classified as "semiconductor devices." The nature of a semiconductor can be explained best by first explaining conductors and nonconductors. Electrons have little difficulty in passing through the materials called conductors such as silver and copper. On the other hand they cannot pass at all through insulators or nonconductors such as glass, mica, silk and polystyrene. The semiconductors are between conductors and nonconductors in the nature of the path they provide for moving electrons (an electric current). Semiconductors offer much resistance to electrons but they do permit some to pass under certain conditions. In other words, semiconductors are neither good conductors nor good insulators.

The principal semiconductors used in the manufacture of transistors are the elements germanium and silicon.

There are two principal types of transistor. One is called a POINT-CONTACT transistor. The other is a JUNCTION transistor.

A point-contact transistor consists of a tiny piece of germanium crystal having two fine pointed wires in contact with its top surface. A third wire connects to the body of the crystal. Point-contact transistors are excellent high-speed switches for electric computers.

The junction-type transistor is used in every branch of electronics. The junction transistor is built like a sandwich with three layers of semiconductor. An inner layer of semiconductor corresponding to the "meat" is enclosed between two outer layers of semiconductor corresponding to the "bread" in a sandwich. The inner layer of semiconductor has electrical characteristics differing from those of the material in the outer layers. A wire terminal is welded to each one of the layers and identified as the emitter, base and collector. When a junction transistor is connected in an electronic circuit, the base electrode corresponds approximately to the grid of a vacuum tube, the emitter to the cathode and the collector to the plate.

Junction transistors are made in two forms—N-P-N and P-N-P. They are quite similar except that the direction of current flow and voltage polarity is reversed.

The transistors used in a radio receiver are required to carry only a fraction of a watt and do not develop any noticeable amount of heat. But those of the "power" type, built to carry considerable current in amplifier, oscillator and other power circuits develop heat which would destroy them unless it is quickly dissipated. "Power" transistors are therefore mounted on a sheet of metal which will radiate the heat into the atmosphere. The metal sheet used for this purpose is termed a "heat sink."

"TELSTAR"—COMMUNICATIONS SATELLITE

Early (3:35 A. M.) on the morning of July 10, 1962, a "Delta" rocket roared upward from its launching pad at Cape Canaveral, Florida. In the nose cone was a 170-pound spherical satellite named "Telstar." The satellite was soon detached from its rocket and went into orbit around the earth (the lowest point, closest to earth, 593 miles and the highest point, farthest from earth, 3,502 miles).

The successful launching of Telstar was the first step in establishing a worldwide radio communications system via a radio relay station orbiting around the earth through space. Telstar worked beautifully. Before the day that Telstar was launched had ended, live television programs, originating in the United States, were successfully beamed to Europe and a live European TV program was seen in millions of American homes. All of this was relayed by Telstar.

Telstar has been called a "microwave tower in the sky." Microwaves are the radiowaves produced by radio-frequency currents which alternate millions of times per second and are used for many forms of communication. A good technical label for Telstar, since it is the first satellite of its kind, is "an experimental microwave repeater satellite." It was designed and built to receive microwave signals from earth stations, amplify them and retransmit them so that they can be picked up at other earth stations thousands of miles away. The communications picked up and retransmitted by Telstar can be those of voice, music, television, data, facsimile or any other form of intelligence ordinarily handled by wire or ground micro-

TELSTAR—THE FIRST COMMUNICATIONS SATELLITE

Solar cells which convert sunlight into electric current and transistors made it possible to build this amazing instrument.

wave systems. In addition to its microwave communications repeater apparatus, the satellite is equipped with:

1. A microwave beacon
2. A very high-frequency beacon transmitter
3. A command receiver telemetry system
4. A solar power plant
5. Apparatus for radiation experiments

This auxiliary equipment reports experimental information, aids the ground stations in tracking the satellite and provides control of its operation from the earth.

Telstar completes each of its orbits around the earth in 157.8 minutes. A simple calculation using this figure shows that nine complete orbits are made in just under 24 hours. The small size of Telstar is amazing. It has a diameter of 34½ inches and is shaped like a ball with seventy-two square or rectangular facets (flat areas) on its surface. Sixty of the facets are covered with silicon solar cells (a total of 3,600 cells) which convert the energy in sunlight to electricity and generate approximately 15 watts of electric current for recharging the storage battery used to power the electronic equipment. The solar cells are protected against abrasion by meteoric dust and particles by strips of synthetic sapphire.

A helical antenna atop the satellite radiates down to earth the telemetry signals which convey information on conditions in the space inside and outside the satellite. The same antenna radiates a coarse beacon signal and also picks up coded command signals from the ground stations which control the communications and telemetry signals. As it orbits, Telstar revolves. This spinning motion gives the satellite stability so that its radio antennas are correctly orientated. While the satellite is in radio contact with the Bell system's earth station at Andover, Maine, it reports 112 important measurements and observations each minute. Telstar reports its own temperature (65 to 70 degrees Fahrenheit) and gives other information useful to the designers of future satellites and to the personnel who will operate the earth stations which will communicate with them.

Semiconductors made it possible to build Telstar. In all the elaborate electronic apparatus enclosed in the satellite, there is only one radio tube but there are 1,464 diodes and 1,064 transistors.

Telstar is the product of many minds and hands. More than 1,200 different companies participated in its creation as subcontractors and suppliers of materials and parts. Bell Telephone Laboratories, Inc. provided the technical leadership and the Bell System underwrote the entire cost of about $50,000,000. The satellite was launched at Cape Canaveral by the National Aeronautics and Space Administration at the Bell System's expense.

Telstar II and other satellites have rocketed into orbit in space since the successful launching of Telstar I. The "Telstar" type is used principally for communication purposes, that is, relaying telephone and television signals overseas between America and Europe and other parts of the earth. The "Tiros" satellites, designed and built by the Radio Corporation of America under contract to the National Aeronautics and Space Administration, are weather satellites. They send continuous television pictures of the large-scale cloud patterns that cover the earth. Weather Bureau meteorologists can thereby study weather as it develops. Weather forecasts become more accurate as scientists see the birth and growth of storms. Advance warnings of hurricanes help to lessen their havoc.

CHAPTER SIXTEEN

ELECTROCHEMISTRY, A KIT OF TOOLS
FOR THE CHEMIST

ONE of the most obliging things about electricity is that many of its tricks are reversible. Magnetism can be used to produce electricity and electricity will produce magnetism. Electricity will produce heat and heat will produce electricity. But that is not all. Just as chemical action, under the right conditions (as Volta discovered when he made the first battery), will generate a current of electricity, so also this wonder may be reversed and a current of electricity made the means of bringing about chemical action. This trick has become one of the most important labors that electricity performs in these scientific days in which we live. Usually we are not aware of it, because the chemical processes in which electricity plays an important part take place in factories where the average person does not see them.

AN ELECTRICAL KIT OF TOOLS FOR THE CHEMIST

One of the best ways to appreciate how electricity is used in chemistry is to liken it to a hammer. A hammer may be used to knock things apart and also to put them together again. Electricity is used to knock chemical compounds apart and also to put them together again. Best of all, electricity will put chemicals together again in new combinations which are never found in nature and the chemist can thus produce many new and useful substances.

At Niagara Falls, where electricity is produced very cheaply by water power, is one of the great centers of the electrochemical industry. In order to describe all the interesting processes of making the thousand and one different chemical substances for which electricity is used we would almost have to change this book into one about chemistry instead of electricity. Here are just a few of the common things which it may surprise you to learn are made by an electrochemical process:

Aluminum   Fertilizers
Carborundum   Special Steels
Chlorine   Graphite
Bleaching Powder

There are two ways of using electricity commercially to pry apart old chemical compounds and build up new ones. One is by sending an electric current through a solution of chemicals and the other is by utilizing the terrific heat of the electric furnace.

THE TERRIFIC HEAT OF THE ELECTRIC FURNACE WILL MAKE DIAMONDS

Heat is one of the most powerful tools that the modern chemist possesses. The early chemists and metallurgists had no hotter fire than that which could be produced by blowing a strong draft of air through burning charcoal. This would produce only a temperature of about 1,000 degrees Fahrenheit, just barely enough for smelting iron and copper. On the other hand, an electric furnace produces a terrific inferno with a temperature of 7,000 to 14,000 degrees Fahrenheit. It is so hot that the feats which it will accomplish are almost like magic. Even miniature diamonds can be made with its aid.

The seething temperatures of an electric arc furnace are produced by the electric arc which Sir Humphry Davy discovered. Davy's tiny arc, fed with the current from a set of Volta's batteries, would seem pitifully small alongside of one of the huge arc furnaces consuming thousands of amperes of current generated by the huge dynamos at Niagara Falls.

SILVER FROM CLAY BY MEANS OF ELECTRICITY

The useful metal called aluminum which we are all familiar with comes from clays and earths, and it was impossible to produce it on a commercial basis until it was discovered how to do it by an electrical process. A mineral called bauxite is the source of our aluminum pots and pans. The bauxite is dissolved in a molten mass of cryolite (a mineral from Greenland) and an electric current sent through it. The result is the lightweight silvery metal used for making pots and pans, automobile crank cases and a thousand and one other things. Once it was called "silver from clay" and sold for $16 to $20 an ounce. This useful metal formerly kept in a glass case and exhibited as a curiosity, now sells for 20 cents a pound and nearly 4,000,000,-000 pounds are smelted every year in the United States.

Graphite is also a product of the electric furnace. This valuable material is an important lubricating material and the principal ingredient of pencil "leads." Another product of the furnace is Carborundum. Perhaps you may think of Carborundum as a material for making stones for sharpening tools, but that is one of its least important uses. The iron and steel parts of all engines, machines, automobiles, etc., which must fit together accurately, are finished by grinding. The grinding is done with artificial abrasives such as Carborundum. Carborundum is made of a mixture of sand, coke, sawdust, and salt. The miracle of electricity and the electric furnace turns these ingredients into a material almost as hard as diamond and of great commercial importance. If all the grinding machinery were removed from modern machine shops and factories where steel must be brought to an accurate size and finish, our whole industrial system would be paralyzed.

THE PATHFINDERS

Two pioneering men named Carlisle and Nicholson were the first to find out that electricity could be used to pry apart chemicals. When Volta succeeded in making his first pile, he wrote to Sir Joseph Banks, President of the Royal Society of England, announcing the new source of electricity. Sir Joseph showed the letter to Carlisle and Nicholson and they immediately set about building one of the new Voltaic piles so that they could experiment with the new wonder. They sent the electric current from a Voltaic pile through water and were amazed to find that the water decomposed into two gases—hydrogen and oxygen. The news spread like wildfire through the scientific world. It soon reached a young chemist in Sweden named Berzelius. Berzelius immediately began to work prying apart other liquids with a Voltaic pile. He made another amazing discovery. He found that metals always went to the positive pole and non-metals to the negative. Here in this simple discovery began the huge science of electrochemistry. The refining of metals, the making of abrasives, electroplating, the manufacture of chlorine, bleaches, fertilizers, and many other valuable chemical compounds and processes grew out of these experiments of Davy, Carlisle, Nicholson, and Berzelius.

In a small book about electricity there is hardly enough space to more than mention electrochemistry. There is a great deal more known about it than you will find in this chapter. Knowledge of it fills many volumes.

CHLORINE—A LIFESAVER PRODUCED BY ELECTRICITY

Only a very few years ago the drinking water in many cities in this country was polluted with typhoid fever germs and thousands of cases of serious illness from this cause occurred every year. Then came the beneficent discovery that a tiny bit of liquid chlorine, less than one drop in fifty gallons of water, or even a small amount of bleaching powder would destroy all the dangerous disease-breeding bacteria. In a short time, the hospitals started to become emptied of typhoid fever cases. The means of prevention is so simple that an epidemic of typhoid is a disgrace to the health authorities of any community that calls itself civilized.

However, preventing typhoid fever is not the only use for liquid chlorine. It is one of the essential ingredients in the process of making dyes, purifying oils, preserving timber, producing gasoline, chloroform, fire extinguishers, and in the preparation of valuable drugs.

Liquid chlorine is made by an electrochemical process. Chlorine is the partner of a metal called sodium and the two together form the little white powder used on the dining table—common salt. Western New York State possesses some great salt mines and their proximity to a source of cheap electric power at Niagara Falls made it possible to develop a huge industry for decomposing salt. The process is very simple. The electric current is passed through tanks of salt dissolved in water and the result is caustic soda, chlorine, and hydrogen.

Caustic soda is used in the production of soap, paper pulp, and for many other purposes.

AN EXPERIMENT IN ELECTROCHEMISTRY

You can perform the experiment of making chlorine, hydrogen, and caustic soda from a salt solution. You will need three dry cells which should be connected in series and two small carbon rods. If you take the carbon rods out of two old flashlight cells, they will do very nicely. Twist a bare copper wire around each of the carbons at the end fitted with the brass cap so as to make a good electrical connection. Fill a glass tumbler with a strong solution of salt water. Connect the carbon rods to the terminals of the battery and place them in the salt-water solution. The rods should be about an inch or so apart. It is important to keep the copper wires and the brass caps out of the solution, only the carbon being immersed.

You will notice tiny bubbles of gas forming on the carbon rods and floating up to the surface. Those rising from the rod connected to the negative terminal of the battery are hydrogen while those from the positive are chlorine. If you hold your nose close to the positive carbon you will be able to notice the peculiar, disagreeable odor of the chlorine.

ELECTROPLATING

Another one of those instances of an electrical action that works both ways is that of electroplating. It is just the reverse of a Voltaic battery wherein a metal disappears into a solution and produces electricity. In electroplating an electric current passing through a

AN EXPERIMENT IN ELECTROCHEMISTRY

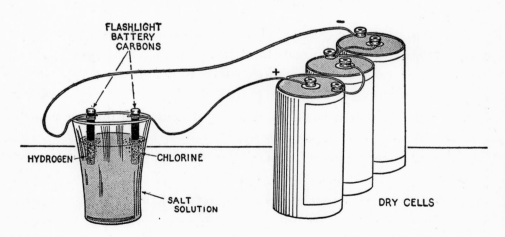

chemical solution causes a metal to appear. It is a magic which is an important part of industry. Water faucets, automobile parts, electrical appliances, sewing machines, and hardware fittings are only a few of the many things which are electroplated with silver, nickel, chromium, or brass to improve their appearance and to prevent rust and tarnish.

A very important use for electroplating is in making the "plates" for printing books, etc. Type metal wears very quickly and the letters become indistinct. The metal is too soft to print many impressions. In order to obtain better printing when running large editions, it is customary to print from "plates" or electrotypes. A mold is made by pressing the type into wax. The wax mold is then coated with graphite and placed in a solution where it is plated with a thin shell of copper. The shell is separated from the wax and then "backed" by pouring molten type metal over the back.

The process of electroplating is a simple one. The articles to be plated are washed and cleaned and hung in a tank containing a solution of copper, nickel, chromium, or whatever metal the coating is to be. They are connected to the negative pole of a "plating" dynamo. A plating dynamo generates a current of low voltage and very high amperage. The positive terminal of the dynamo is connected to an electrode called the "anode," a sheet of copper, nickel, chromium, or whatever metal the coating is to be. When the current is turned on, metal from the anode disappears into the solution and reappears on the articles to be plated. When the coating is thick enough, the articles are taken out and polished on a buffing wheel.

CHAPTER SEVENTEEN

MISCELLANEOUS USES OF ELECTRICITY

X-RAYS

THE discovery of that invisible penetrating light called the X-ray, which passes through solid objects, placed in the hands of doctors an instrument of the greatest value in remedying pain and suffering. X-rays have become a window of the body through which the trained specialist can look to see that which heretofore had been hidden from his eyes without an operation. At first, this wonderful gift of science was used only to locate bullets and splinters of metal embedded in the body or objects which had been accidentally swallowed, and to examine broken bones. Now appendicitis, gall-bladder troubles, tuberculosis, tumors, infected teeth, and many other ailments can be diagnosed by the shadows in an X-ray photograph.

THE COOLIDGE TUBE

This modern tube has entirely replaced the old-fashioned X-ray tube and made it possible to make X-ray pictures almost as easily as ordinary snapshots may be taken with a Kodak.

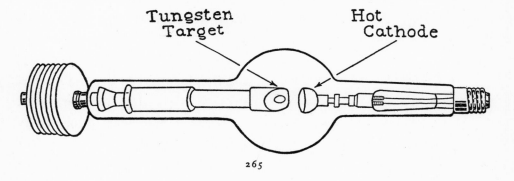

Tungsten Target

Hot Cathode

Many human ailments are easily revealed to the expert eye of the radiologist.

X-rays were first observed by a brilliant scientist named Sir William Crookes, but he did not find out how to put them to any practical use, and thought that he had discovered a new form of matter which he called radiant matter.

The investigation which brought the discovery that the rays would pass through solid objects and which gave them their name were the experiments of a pleasant and friendly man, William Conrad Roentgen, Professor of Physics at the University of Württemberg. In December, 1895, Professor Roentgen announced that, while experimenting with some vacuum tubes, he had discovered a new ray, which he called X-rays because their nature was then unknown. His experiments were immediately repeated in laboratories in Europe and America. Within three months after their real discovery by Roentgen, X-rays were being put to practical use in a hospital in Vienna in connection with surgical operations.

Until a few years ago, X-ray tubes (called Crookes tubes after

A POWERFUL COOLIDGE TUBE

This type of tube is for giving X-ray treatments. The tube is oil-cooled and mounted on an adjustable stand. The invisible light from an X-ray tube is a treatment for certain ailments as well as a means of making photographs of the interior of the body.

MAGNETISM

When electricity flows through a coil

HEAT
LIGHT

When electricity
meets resistance

CHEMICAL
CHANGE

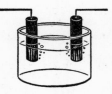

When electricity
passes through
solutions

INDUCED
CURRENTS

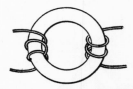

In a coil when a
nearby coil is
electrified or
de-electrified

LIGHT
RAYS

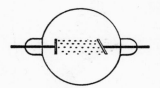

When electricity
passes through a
vacuum

ELECTRICITY'S ACTIVITIES

Almost all electrical devices depend on one or more of the effects
produced by an electric current which are illustrated above.

the famous experimenter whose work was the forerunner of Roentgen's discovery) were very unreliable. But Doctor Coolidge, an expert of the General Electric Company, and Lilienfeld in Germany produced a new type of tube called a "hot-cathode" tube which made the taking of X-ray pictures a much simpler matter. The tubes which doctors and dentists use nowadays are Coolidge tubes.

The use of X-rays in medical and surgical work has been so spectacular that it has overshadowed the fact that there are many other applications of great importance. These are in the field of industry and commerce where X-rays have greatly aided laboratory and research work and in the factory where they are used to test for flaws and unseen cracks in castings and forgings.

ELECTRIC CLOCKS

It is easy to always have correct time wherever there is an alternating-current supply generated at a public power station. An electric clock may be "geared" to the unvarying dynamos. The speed

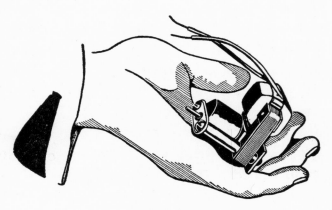

CLOCK MOTOR

The tiny motor in a Telechron clock bears the same relation to the huge motors in an electric locomotive as the minnow does to a whale. They work on the same principle.

of the huge generators is so closely regulated that it never varies a fraction of a second. It seems almost inconceivable to connect the tiny wheels of a clock to the massive generators in a power house but a way has been found to use the pulsating alternations of the electric-lighting current to drive a clock motor. The motor is so made that it does not gain or lose so much as one revolution. You may have wondered what makes an electrical clock go and keep accurate time since it has no springs, weights, or escapements like an ordinary clock. A tiny synchronous motor (synchronous means happening at the same rate) drives the hands of the clock. There are two types of the little motors used. Those in the higher-priced and better elec-tric clocks use a "Telechron" motor which is self-starting and will run many years without any attention whatsoever. A much cheaper motor which must be given a twist to start is used in the low-priced clocks sold in drug stores and on bargain counters.

RECTIFIERS—DEVICES FOR CHANGING ALTERNATING CURRENT INTO DIRECT CURRENT

Some electrical devices require direct current for their operation. Storage batteries can be charged only by direct current. Radar ap-paratus, radio and television transmitters and receivers, magnetic chucks in machine shops, electroplating and electrochemical proc-esses all utilize direct current. Since the 120-volt light and power supply is almost universally alternating current it cannot be used for these purposes without being rectified, that is, changed from AC to DC. This can be accomplished by a motor-generator or one of the devices termed a "rectifier." The type of device used depends upon the amount of current to be rectified. A motor generator is a combination of an alternating-current motor coupled to a direct-current generator. The motor drives the generator and the latter produces the direct current desired. Rectifiers are all "electrical valves." They might be termed "one way streets for electrons." They allow an electric current to pass in one direction but not in the other. Radio tubes have a rectifying action. In fact, radio tubes are called "valves" in Great Britain. Selenium and silicon, copper oxide, mercury vapor, argon, neon, hydrogen and xenon can be used as rectifiers. Selenium, silicon, and copper oxide require proper chemical preparation before they will serve as efficient rectifiers.

Automobile service stations usually obtain direct current for battery charging from a motor-generator, a selenium rectifier or a Tungar bulb. The Tungar bulb also has the imposing name of "hot-cathode gas-filled rectifier." Inside the bulb is a heavy filament of

RECTIFIER

Tungar and Rectigon bulbs used to change AC to DC for charging storage batteries are filled with rarefied argon gas. When the filament is lighted an electric current will pass in one direction only: between the filament and the electrode.

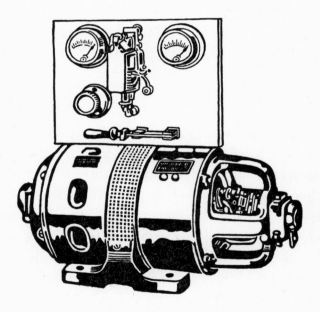

A MOTOR-GENERATOR

This is a combination of a motor and a generator which is used in battery-charging stations. The motor runs on alternating current and drives the generator which produces direct current.

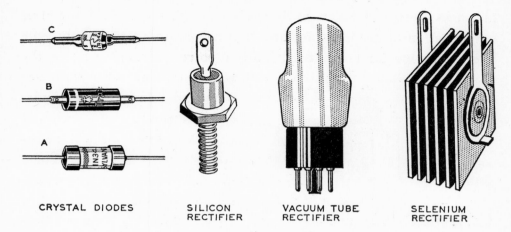

CRYSTAL DIODES   SILICON RECTIFIER   VACUUM TUBE RECTIFIER   SELENIUM RECTIFIER

FOUR VARIETIES OF SMALL RECTIFIER

A, B and C are diode rectifiers. They are commonly used as detectors in small radio receivers. D is a silicon power rectifier. E is a vacuum tube rectifier used to produce direct current for the plate circuits of radio receivers. F is a small selenium rectifier.

tungsten wire called the cathode and right above it a small disk of graphite called the anode. Current can pass from the cathode to the anode but not pass in the opposite direction.

The silicon, galena and germanium crystals often used by boys as detectors in a homemade radio receiver are small valves which rectify the alternating current generated in the antenna by incoming waves.

ELECTRIC ELEVATORS

Tall buildings would not be very practical without elevators. Surely no one would want to climb more than three or four flights of stairs to go to bed, make a business call, or visit friends.

The first passenger elevator was operated by steam. It was built by Otis Tufts in 1859 for what was then the new Fifth Avenue

Hotel in New York City. Only two such elevators were built. The other was installed in a building in Philadelphia. Then came the hydraulic elevator (operated by water power). You have seen the

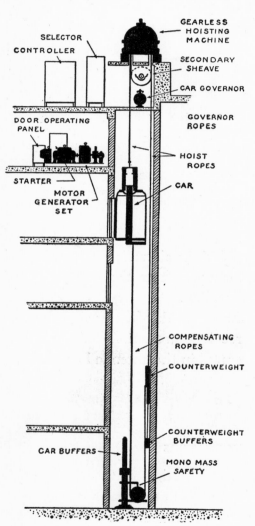

principle of the hydraulic elevator used in gasoline service stations to raise automobiles so that the under parts can be inspected and greased. There are still a few hydraulic passenger elevators in service but they belong to the past. Electricity has replaced water.

The modern high-speed electric elevator is a wonderful machine that has been developed and improved until it is almost perfect. There has never been a fatal accident due to machinery failure in a modern electric traction elevator since the machine was first developed in 1902. The steel hoisting ropes which raise and lower the car pass around a drum or "driving sheave" on an extremely slow speed motor turning over but 95 revolutions per minute. The motor is built especially for elevator service and operates only on direct current. To control the

From "The Story of Skyscrapers." By permission.

A COMPLETE ELECTRIC
ELEVATOR SYSTEM

heavy current necessary for operation of the motor would require switches of great capacity if the problem had not been solved in a very clever way. The switch on the elevator which the operator moves to stop and start the car does not control the hoisting motor directly but sets a "control panel" into operation. The control panel is located somewhere near the motor and contains a great many different switches, relays and protective devices, all automatic in action.

Electric elevators have made it practicable to have an office a thousand feet above the street level. Every day many millions of people go soaring up and down in countless elevators operated by electric motors. Modern high-speed elevators use a direct-current motor.

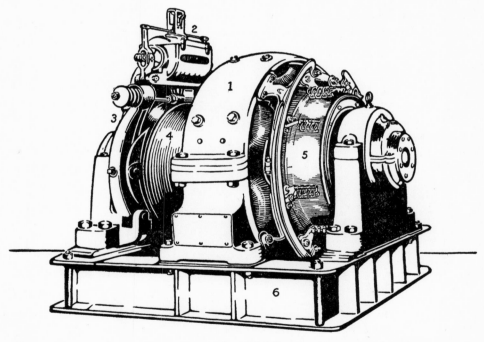

From "The Story of Skyscrapers." By Alfred P. Morgan.

THE OTIS GEARLESS ELEVATOR MOTOR

Some of the parts of this motor may be identified as follows: 1 is the frame. 2 is the brake mechanism. 3 is the brake band. 4 is the cable drum. 5 is the commutator. 6 is the bed.

INDEX